PRAISE FOR
Scenes from a Criminal Lawyer's Notebook

"Gregg Naclerio is a born storyteller! You can hear his unique voice as he pulls you into each tale of his time as a criminal lawyer. You can't wait to hear how each story turns out as he weaves the web of lies and half-truths that constitute these amazing stories. He is correct, you can't make this stuff up! I know you will enjoy these yarns as much as I did."

— **Robin Lane**, MEd, retired educator

"I can honestly say I enjoyed reading this book as much as I enjoy those by David Baldacci and Lee Child. The stories are interesting, and reading them was like learning law from the inside out. It was a quick and entertaining read."

— **Dan Marusa**, retired, US Navy

"Once again, Gregg Naclerio has treated us to his recollections of his interesting and entertaining criminal law war stories."

— **Maryann Wolf**

"I had the great privilege to have a sneak preview of *Scenes from a Criminal Lawyer's Notebook: Cases You Can't Make Up*. Gregg Naclerio's experience proves life is always better than fiction. Read this book!"

— **Carolyn Holcomb Hirso**, The NC Real Estate Firm

"J.K Rowling once observed, 'There's always room for a story that can transport people to another place.' Gregg Naclerio brilliantly transports his readers through a fascinating world of criminal behavior in the business world and entices his reader to see how—in the end—criminals can and should be held accountable, all with a delightful dash of humor along the way."

—**George A. Higgins**, retired major general, US Army

"Reading this book will give you a sense of the legal skill and experience necessary to successfully try (and win) cases, connect with clients and all parties involved, and explain the legal lingo (for us lay-people) which has helped to make this book so much more enjoyable to read. Gregg also issues a compelling recommendation for you to tell (write) your own story for a future generations to read, including tips for getting started."

—**Patrick Service**, certified exercise physiologist

SCENES FROM A CRIMINAL LAWYER'S NOTEBOOK

CASES YOU CAN'T MAKE UP

GREGG NACLERIO

LYSTRA BOOKS
& Literary Services

Fifty percent of the profit of this book will be donated to the Jimmy V Foundation for Cancer Research, located in Cary, North Carolina.

Scenes From a Criminal Lawyer's Notebook:
Cases You Can't Make Up
Copyright © 2025 by Gregg Naclerio
All rights reserved

ISBN paperback 979-8-9921363-1-9
ISBN ebook 979-8-9921363-2-6
Library of Congress Control Number: 2025907190

The contents of this book are the intellectual property of Gregg Naclerio. Except for brief excerpts for reviews, no portion of the text may be reproduced in any form without written permission from the author or publisher. Contact the publisher at the address below.

Book design by Kelly Prelipp Lojk

Author's photo by Sean Gregory

Published by Lystra Books & Literary Services, LLC
391 Lystra Estates Drive, Chapel Hill, NC 27517
lystrabooks@gmail.com

*To my grandparents
Gregorio, Teresa, Columbo and Matilda
for the courage to leave their homes in Italy*

CONTENTS

Preface xi

1 Hog-Tied in the Palace 1

2 Building the Medicaid Fraud Highway . . . 36

    Part I: Medicaid Fraud 37
        The One-Lane Road 38
        Ultraviolet Cabinets 44
        Physical Therapists 45
        Blood Testing Labs 46
        The Two-Lane Boulevard 51
        The Four-Lane Parkway 53

    Part II: Automobile Insurance Fraud . . 57
        The Six-Lane Expressway 57

3	Cases from a Defense Attorney's Files	75
	Does an MRI Exam Hurt?	75
	Sometimes It Happens	92
	To Pee or Not to Pee, That Is the Question	99
4	Divine Justice	104
5	Did I Tell You About…?	124
	The Case of the Chapel Cover-Up	124
	Learning the Lingo	130
	The Human Lie Detector	131
	Observe by Watching	139
6	Revenge Is a Dish Best Served Cold	147
7	Who Can You Trust?	167
	The Bank Trust Officer?	167
	A Dying Lady?	178
	A Fire Insurance Broker?	185

8 **Need a License to Steal?
   Own a Hospital** *193*
   Four Years Later *235*

9 **Things Are Not Always as They Seem** . . . *237*
   The Priest's Tale. *238*
   Looking for Love in All the
   Wrong Places *241*
   'An Act of Kindness,
   No Matter How Small,
   Is Never Wasted' –*Aesop* *245*

10 **There Is an Author Inside of You** *256*

PREFACE

Hey, thanks to all of you who have come back after reading my first book, *You Can't Make This Stuff Up: My Criminal Law War Stories*. It was your requests for additional stories that prompted this second book. To new readers, I'm glad you decided to join us because I am about to take you on an adventure to see firsthand what it's like to practice criminal law.

Being a criminal law trial attorney is best described in one word—"thrilling." You never know what awaits you at the other end of the phone or across your desk. The one thing you do know is that the person you are speaking to is having one of the worst days of his or her life.

If you are a prosecutor, your task is to protect the public, often those most vulnerable, from all types of miscreants and secure justice for those the criminal justice system labels "victims."

If you are a defense attorney, your client faces the loss of family, job, reputation, and possibly freedom.

My goal is to take you behind the headlines of a criminal case and give you a peek into what it's like to investigate, defend or prosecute a criminal case. A criminal case is more than a collection of cold hard facts. It's full of emotions as well. As I peel back the cover of the criminal case, you will meet victims, defendants, police officers, judges, prosecutors, defense attorneys, and others, all strangers to each other until one event causes their lives to collide on a road to that elusive goal of Justice. A concept one philosopher defined as "God's idea – Man's ideal." Additionally, you may even learn a thing or two about the criminal law.

As is often true in life, real events are more fascinating than those made up by fiction writers like Patterson, Turow or Baldacci. The stories I am about to tell you actually happened. Even though most of the cases received attention in the local press and many of the people involved have departed this world, I have changed their names. I am sure I have forgotten some facts of each case, and at times I had to make some things up to have the tales flow. Likewise, the transcripts and conversations I share with you are true representations but are not necessarily verbatim.

Let's call these "semi-true stories." And isn't that true enough?

If I have done my job correctly, you'll be able to feel and share the same emotions I went through in each case. Some of the memories contained herein are sad, some funny and some just downright unbelievable; yet all of us who have engaged in the combat of practicing criminal law have war stories. These are mine.

So, buckle your seatbelts, make sure your seat-back tray is in its full upright and locked position, because

I'm going to take you on a flight to discover what it's really like to practice criminal law.

I wrote this book, as I did the first book, to share my stories and to pay forward, in some small way, the blessings my family and I have received. Therefore, fifty percent of my royalties from the sale of this book will be donated to the Jimmy V Foundation for Cancer Research, located in Cary, North Carolina.

CHAPTER ONE

Hog-Tied in the Palace

Deputy Director Yanni Pappas and I were engaged in an animated discussion. In truth, it was a heated argument concerning which of our heritages contributed more to the advancement of Western civilization: the ancient Greeks represented by Aristotle and Socrates or the Italian Renaissance of Michelangelo and Leonardo. Fortunately, we were interrupted by Senior Investigator Jack Keys who charged into my office without his customary courtesy knock.

"We just got a call on the Patient Abuse Hotline," he reported.

In the summer of 1986, I was a special assistant attorney general with the New York State Office of the Special Prosecutor for Nursing Homes, covering the Long Island region. When a call about abuse came in, it went to Jack. He was our lead patient abuse investigator and also a registered nurse.

It was our office's protocol that the lead investigator and the assigned assistant attorney general (it was me that month) would respond immediately to the scene of the alleged abuse. By having a seasoned investigator and prosecutor respond at the same time, evidence could be collected, preserved and evaluated in real time and a decision to arrest a suspect or not could be made without delay.

But when I stood up to grab my jacket, Jack inexplicably sat down. I looked at him as if to say, "let's go!" but before I could mouth the words he responded, "No rush on this one, boss. The victim—if she is in fact a victim—has been dead and buried for several weeks."

That was my introduction to Alice Hightower, a resident at The Palace Family Care Home, situated fifteen miles from our office.

As the regional director, I was certainly familiar with nursing homes, health-related facilities, and adult homes, but I never heard of a "family care home." And even though I must have driven by it on Route 25A on my way to Port Jefferson Village over a hundred times, I had never noticed The Palace from the road or any signage pointing to its location.

The Palace was located on a two-acre parcel in Setauket, in Suffolk County, surrounded by the Gold Coast neighborhoods of Old Field, Strongs Neck, Poquott and Belle Terre. Residents of these neighborhoods generally traveled to New York City to work on Wall Street or at national corporations in Midtown. One resident, the owner of a major brokerage firm, even took a seaplane from his back yard dock to Wall

Street every day. Others were physicians who treated their patients at one of three community hospitals or at the state university medical center. Still others taught at Stony Brook University or owned businesses on Long Island.

Their kids played sports or instruments and moms carpooled to every imaginable after-school activity. Social events or dinner parties were regular occurrences, and the residents spent part of every weekend at the Old Field or Harbor Hills Clubs to both unwind and hunt for new business contacts. They enjoyed the good life in their ritzy ghetto.

Whether one is rich, poor, or somewhere in the middle, most people will be faced with caring for elderly relatives—most likely mom or dad. Caring for an elderly parent is something most people are not prepared to do or, quite frankly, willing to do. It is hard to change your lifestyle when you find dad cannot take care of himself and you are faced with making several trips a week to help him manage or moving him in with you, your spouse and your four teenage kids. I have been there, and it is not fun. Whether you are retired or working, becoming a caregiver is not easy, and few of us are prepared.

That is the primary reason why facilities like nursing homes, adult homes and assisted living communities flourish. If you have the money, some of your guilt can be expiated by finding an upscale place for dad and mom. The Palace Family Care Home was one such place. The Palace was not a "facility" under New York state law because it did not "render care" to its residents and as such was not licensed by any governmental agency.

People learned about it by word of mouth among the wealthy. A golfing buddy or bridge club friend might listen to your constant whining about your dad and then suggest you contact The Palace for a tour. You do so. We will tag along.

The house was situated on a half-acre property just fifty yards to the north of the home where its owner Aurora March lived. While Aurora's home was a two-story custom-built farmhouse, the dwelling used as The Palace was a sprawling ranch. It was landscaped just like her home and had a winding driveway two cars wide leading to the main entrance. Its exterior was well-maintained, painted a desert tan color and was no more than fifteen years old.

You enter The Palace through large double doors and step into a large well-appointed foyer where Aurora March herself greets you. Standing ramrod straight, the five feet eight, forty-one-year-old bleach blonde looks just like one of those flashy real estate agents featured in the magazines selling million-dollar-plus mansions. She is dressed impeccably and wears small but noticeable diamond stud earrings as if she were going to an elegant dinner party even though it's 1 p.m. on a Thursday. You have no doubt in your mind that you are speaking to the person in charge even before two of the obsequious staff who are at least twenty years her senior address her as Ms. March.

As she takes a moment to direct her staff, you can't help but notice the highly polished white oak floors that you were told run throughout the home. You have a fleeting thought that these floors look too highly polished to be safe for its elderly occupants, but the thought vanishes quickly as you see immediately to the right a library room with built-in maple bookcases, plush carpet and decorated with antique furniture and accessories. The room looks like it belongs in a museum. All that is missing is the red velvet rope across the threshold.

The dining space on the opposite side of the hallway is about three times that of an average dining room. The bottom third of each wall is wainscoted and topped by soft blue wallpaper. A gold-colored chandelier hangs over the center of the six-foot-long solid walnut table. Six large and comfortable looking chairs surround the table. Adjacent to the dining room is the large kitchen featuring all Sub-Zero equipment and a commercial-size gas range. Across the hall is the great room with a state-of-the-art television and an impressive fireplace with a large hand-carved mantle. Leather recliners and two couches are strategically placed for viewing the TV or enjoying conversation. Indeed on this day, three of the five residents are watching *The $25,000 Pyramid* while the other two are chatting with a staff member. Sliding glass doors provide access to the outside covered patio.

Continuing towards the rear of the house, you see The Palace's five bedrooms. Ms. March tells you that every two bedrooms share a cozy living room space and a full bath. The fifth bedroom has a private living room and full bath. As you peek into each bedroom, you note they are all nicely furnished such as you would expect at a fancy hotel. All of them have queen beds except for one room with two single beds, one on each wall. The rooms are spacious, and the personal furniture and the bedding reflect the taste of each occupant or their family. Your tour concludes back in the kitchen where, over a glass of red wine, Ms. March tells you of her philosophy of care.

"The Palace is not a medical facility. We provide no nursing care. We have your family members come to live in my house just as if they were living in your house. During the day, we have a staff of local Port Jefferson women we affectionately call The Ladies who enjoy working with the elderly and are happy to make some extra spending money. They prepare three homecooked meals each day plus an afternoon snack. At night, my family and I are just down the road. Our staffing ratio is one of The Ladies to every two residents, which when compared to assisted living homes in the area, is markedly higher. In short, we take your place in caring for your loved one."

While the monthly rent was rather steep, it did not cause Aurora March to want for residents. Due to the outstanding reputation The Palace had in the community, Ms. March kept a steady waiting list. That reputation was about to suddenly change.

The hotline call Jack received was from Kathy Vasco, a registered nurse at Stony Brook University Hospital's

Intensive Care Unit (ICU). Kathy said she had been agonizing about whether to call our office for the past two weeks. She reiterated she did not want to make a complaint but wanted to tell us what she had seen that was deeply troubling her.

She agreed to meet with Jack that very afternoon when her shift ended at five-thirty, and I was going to join the meeting. When we met Kathy, she appeared to be about fifty years old, thin and perhaps five feet two at most. She had been a nurse for over twenty-five years and had worked in the ICU for the past four. Kathy said that on August 6, 1986, she was working the day shift when a new patient was brought to her unit from the ER. The patient was the eighty-five-year-old Alice Pruitt Hightower.

"She looked like someone you would see in the photos of World War II concentration camp victims," Kathy told us in a voice filled with pain.

It was this image of her patient that was haunting Kathy.

When Alice arrived at the ICU, she was having trouble breathing despite receiving pure oxygen through a mask around her mouth and nose. Kathy said the patient appeared to be in such discomfort she wanted to get Alice into a bed and start IVs flowing as soon as possible. Without waiting for assistance, Kathy pulled Alice off the gurney onto the bed by herself. We must have looked surprised by Kathy's revelation because she said, "I may only weigh 105 pounds, but Alice was very easy to move. It was like she weighed nothing."

Then in a noticeably slow, almost painful cadence Kathy continued, "I connected Alice to a heart monitor, and as I was setting up her IV-line, Alice said to me, 'dry.' I gave her a cup of water, and she slowly drank about half of it. I then set up the bedside table with a box of tissues. I moved to the head of the bed to titrate her IV fluids, and Alice slowly raised her right arm and placed it on the table. Then I saw her use what strength she had to pull a Kleenex out of the box. I thought she was going to use the tissue to wipe her face, but she placed it in her mouth and started to eat it. I stopped her from doing so, and she just looked at me with pleading eyes. She could not speak, but she tried to fight me for the tissue. She was starving and wanted to eat anything. My experience over years of nursing told me Alice was not someone who was demented but struggling to live. I immediately left the room to find the resident, and when I returned about four minutes later, her heart monitor showed a flat line.

"There was nothing more we could do. Alice had died."

Kathy had tears in her eyes. She regained her composure. "After a doctor pronounced her dead, I got the standard pack, which we use to prepare the body for transport to the morgue. Part of that process is to remove all IV lines and wash the body. As I was bathing Alice, I turned her onto her side and noted two decubitus ulcers. The one on her shoulder was at stage three. The other was on her sacrum, her tailbone. I would classify it as stage four."

What's a 'Decubitus'?

A decubitus ulcer, more commonly referred to as a bed sore, is an open wound in the skin. In a stage one ulcer, the skin is discolored and red but not broken. At stage two, the skin breaks open, creating a lesion that resembles an abrasion or popped blister. Stage three occurs when the lesion starts to form a small crater and fat begins to show in the open sore. This type of ulcer opens the body to the possibility of infection, including sepsis. At stage four, the skin and fat layers are breached, and the wound exposes muscle and bone. Damage to deeper tissues, including nerves and tendons, occurs. A stage four decubitus ulcer has potentially life-threatening complications.

Prolonged pressure is the main cause of a decubitus ulcer. Having any patient lie on the same part of the body for a protracted period without being turned to relieve the pressure, along with poor circulation and nutrition, are the main reasons pressure ulcers occur. Patients who are incontinent also have a greater chance of infecting their pressure ulcers.

Generally, most pressure sores are preventable, and the fact that a person has significant decubitus ulcers is a sign of poor patient care.

Kathy said the transfer sheet from the emergency room did not note the presence of any ulcers. When she went to the ER to ask about that, the ER physician said the patient was in such poor condition he did not turn her to examine her back because he wanted to get her into ICU stat, as quickly as possible.

Kathy apologized about not having more information to provide, but she felt it was better that someone in authority be made aware of what she had seen. She had no proof of anything criminal, only a nagging feeling that Alice was trying to tell her something.

She did not want to let Alice down.

After hearing Kathy's account, Jack and I felt there existed enough reasonable suspicion of a possible crime to open an investigation into what caused Alice's death and whether her treatment at The Palace led to her demise. I decided that Jack and I would start working on the Alice Hightower case while Investigator Marc G. Jager led our investigation into The Palace.

Our first task was to interview Alice's next of kin, her brother Stewart Pruitt. This turned out to be a bit of a challenge as Mr. Pruitt had moved to Yorkshire, England, about ten years earlier. He only returned to the States for summer vacations in Southampton. On his last visit to Long Island, Mr. Pruitt, himself seventy-six years old, noticed his eldest sister had begun to physically deteriorate. Alice asked Stewart to take over her considerable finances and to find a place for her to live, a place where "I will not be alone."

Before that request, Alice had lived alone and had fallen twice in the previous three months. The second time Alice remained on the kitchen floor for several hours, unable to get up on her own, until a neighbor heard her cries for help.

Thanks to Stewart's contacts on Long Island, he was able to meet Aurora March, and both he and Alice visited The Palace. After being wait-listed for several months, Alice moved in on January 5, 1986. Thereafter, Stewart and Alice stayed in contact via letters (that's right, no email or Zoom back then) and the occasional telephone call. Stewart also reported that the following month Alice suffered a stroke and was admitted to Stony Brook University Hospital. As a result of the stroke, Alice needed a walker to get around, and more critically, Alice's speech was affected. She suffered from a condition known as aphasia, which meant her speech and comprehension were impaired. She could speak, but her words and sentences did not make sense. When she was discharged from the hospital in mid-February, Alice returned to The Palace.

Six months later, Stewart received word Alice had passed, and he decided that she should be buried in the family plot in Farmingdale. Due to poor health, he was unable to attend the funeral service.

After we obtained the necessary background information, I prepared a subpoena for the medical records of Alice's final hospital admission. When Keys reviewed the medical records, he told me that upon her hospital discharge on February 14, Alice weighed

142 pounds, and on her final admission on August 6, she weighed only 83 pounds—a 59-pound weight loss in less than six months. The final discharge summary also confirmed the two decubitus ulcers noted by Nurse Vasco.

By the end of August, Investigators Keys and Jager had conducted background checks of both The Palace and Ms. March, and they made the decision to interview her about the Alice Hightower matter. Ms. March flatly refused an invitation to come to our office and insisted that any interview be done at The Palace. This was perfectly fine with us. We always preferred to conduct interviews on the subject's premises as opposed to our sterile offices because you never knew what you would find out being on site.

At the appointed time, Ms. March met the investigators at The Palace's front door and gave them the same tour she gave to all prospective residents and their families. The initial meeting lasted about an hour. Jack then asked if they could speak to two of The Ladies that Ms. March said had cared for Alice.

While they were being located, Jager asked where he could go for a smoke break. During the three years they were partners, as a registered nurse, Keys had tried repeatedly to get Jager to stop smoking. His success was limited because Jager now smoked Marlboro Lights instead of unfiltered Camels and agreed to not smoke anytime they were in the same car.

Ms. March apparently objected to smoking as well and sternly advised Jager that there was "no smoking allowed anywhere in The Palace," but he could go out to the patio on the side of the house that she had designated as the "smoking parlor."

In the business of prosecuting crimes, there are times when a case breaks as the result of a fortuitous event, as you will see in several of the cases that follow. Sometimes coincidence or fate or karma intervene. This was one such day. As Jager went out into the smoking parlor, he saw an elderly man standing by a planter that doubled as an ashtray. Jager approached the man and asked for a light even though his father's old Zippo lighter resided in its usual place in his back pocket. Jager had twenty-two years of police experience, mostly as a robbery squad detective, and knew smokers like to talk as they puff. As he accepted the matchbook, he introduced himself and asked the man's name.

The individual, who appeared to be in his late seventies, declined to provide his name or confirm he was a resident. Upon being told that Jager was investigating a case of possible patient abuse, the individual responded he "hated cops" and added, "The old folks here need more help than I can give them."

The individual then refused to say anything more and walked away.

Jager wrote a report of his interviews, and the case started rolling. Here are the highlights.

- ✦ Ms. March advised that Alice Hightower resided in Bedroom 5, which had a private bath. The

Ladies who usually cared for Alice were Dorothea Halloran and Margie Sherill.
✦ Prior to her stroke, Alice participated in the various activities conducted in the great room and dining area but since her stroke she had remained in her room and most of that time in bed.
✦ Ms. March pointed out and repeated several times that The Palace was not a medical facility and as such did not provide medical care to its residents. The only assistance provided was with the activities of daily living like help with toileting, dressing and meal preparation. Accordingly, no doctor had seen Alice since her return from the hospital, and Ms. March reiterated that it was the family's responsibility to provide for medical care.
✦ Both Halloran and Sherill seemed to be afraid of speaking in front of Ms. March, who insisted on being present during all the staff interviews. Dorothea Halloran seemed particularly agitated by questions concerning Alice Hightower.

It took until September 19 to obtain authorization from our city office and for the county court to impanel a special grand jury to investigate the circumstances surrounding the death of Alice Hightower.

The Grand Jury

A grand jury is very different from the trial jury that you may be familiar with. While the trial jury is composed of twelve members and determines guilt or innocence, a grand jury is composed of sixteen to twenty-three individuals who hear evidence to determine if there is reasonable cause to believe a crime was committed and who committed the crime.

The result of a trial jury is a verdict, while the grand jury decides whether to return an indictment charging an individual with a crime.

We determined that we would open the grand jury investigation by having Alice's medical records placed in evidence, followed by testimony from nurse Kathy Vasco and the two women who cared for her at The Palace—Dorothea Halloran and Margie Sherill. Jager was tasked to serve a grand jury subpoena on each of the women. He struck out with Margie, who was spending the winter with her daughter in Cary, North Carolina, but hit a home run when he spoke with Dorothea. Jager just intended to serve the subpoena on Dorothea, which would take all of five minutes, but wound up staying with her for well over an hour.

While still at her residence, Jager called me and said Dorothea wanted to speak to me, A meeting was set for eight o'clock the next morning.

I arrived at my office at 7:30 to find Jager and Dorothea already in the conference room. They made a strange looking couple. Dorothea was in her mid-sixties, and her white hair was pulled high on her head. She had a round cherubic face, and if you wanted a poster for America's Mother, you would pick her for the role in a moment. Jager, on the other hand, was forty-five years old, completely bald, and always had a stern countenance. He could have taken the Telly Savalas role of Detective Theo Kojak in the 1970s TV series. (The running joke in the office was that Jager could—when he wanted to—intimidate a witness even if he said "fluffy bunnies and teddy bears.")

As she sipped her tea, Dorothea told us that in September 1995 she retired from the Town of Huntington after working thirty-two years as a cafeteria supervisor at Bay High School. By January, Dorothea got tired of staying at home and carpooling her grandsons to school. That's when she started working at The Palace. Dorothea worked the breakfast shift (6 a.m. to 10 a.m.) and then returned for the dinner shift (5 p.m. to 8 p.m.) Sunday through Thursday. At that time there were six residents: Alice Hightower; Francine Blackton, who shared a room with Rita Keeler; Stella Baldwin; Atillio Del Negro and Johnny Drinkwater.

Let's listen in on a portion of Jager's interview with Dorothea.

Q: Dorothea, did you have any experience in the healthcare area prior to working at The Palace?

A: No.

Q: Who gave you directions concerning your duties at The Palace?

A: Since I never worked caring for elderly folk except for my dad, I scrupulously followed the directions I got from Ms. March.

Q: What did you do when you got to The Palace at six in the morning?

A: It was the same thing every day I worked. I would get there at about 5:45 and unlock the front door. Then I would go to each resident's room to untie the Gentle Reminders.

Q: What's a Gentle Reminder?

A: That's what Ms. March called them. Each night before she went to her home at 7 p.m., Ms. March and another lady, usually me, would go to each resident's room and put one of the Gentle Reminders on the resident's wrist or ankle or both and then tie the opposite end to the bed spring. This is what I was so upset about … how we tied them in bed each night. God forgive me.

Dorothea started to sob. Jager, completely out of character, reached out and held her hand.

Q: Dorothea, we need you to stay calm and tell us what exactly is a Gentle Reminder?

A: At one end, it has a cuff about three inches wide.

The cuff is lined with lambswool to protect the resident's skin. The cuff goes around the resident's wrist or ankle and the other end gets tied to the bedspring. Ms. March would always tell us to do the ankle and wrist on the same side.

Q: Did you ever place a Gentle Reminder on a resident?

A: (*sobbing*) Yes, several times.

Q: Who told you to use the Gentle Reminders?

A: Ms. March.

Q: Did Ms. March tell you the reason for use of the Gentle Reminders?

A: Yes. She said it reminded the residents not to get out of bed at night since no one was there during the nighttime hours to help them if they fell. In reality, I think it was more than a reminder. They could not get out of bed.

Q: Did all the residents get Gentle Reminders?

A: Only the residents Ms. March thought could get out of bed got them. Usually that was Del Negro, Drinkwater, Stella Baldwin and Francine Blackton. Rita Keller was always in her bed and needed the help of two of us to get into a chair. She did not need one. Neither did Alice Hightower at the end.

Keys, who by now had joined the meeting, asked some questions.

Q: Dorothea, please tell us about Alice Hightower.

A: When Alice returned to The Palace from the

hospital in February, she had to use a walker because of her stroke. Even with the walker, she just shuffled her feet and would stumble walking from her room to the dining area. She came back to us confused and couldn't speak. This one day, it was my son's birthday so I remember it was March 13, I found Alice in the library room. Residents were forbidden to go into that room because Ms. March said the room was just for showing her antiques collection. When I saw Alice in the library, I told her to come out and she started to, but then she stumbled and reached out to grab the end table to stop herself from falling. She grabbed for the tabletop, but she got a lace doily instead and pulled Ms. March's antique Tiffany lamp off the table. The lamp fell, and the stained-glass shade broke in a million pieces. Ms. March heard the crash and came running to the library, where she saw Alice. She was livid. She told me to take Alice immediately to her room and that she was not allowed to come out of her room as she was a danger to herself and other residents. From that day forward, Alice stayed in her room and got all her meals in the room, and she stayed in that room until she died.

Q: Tell Gregg about Alice's meals.

A: God forgive me ... *(crying)* I should have saved her but did not know what to do ...

Dorothea was so upset that we needed to take a break. In an attempt to put her at ease, I told her that since she was being subpoenaed to testify before the grand jury, she would receive transactional immunity for anything she testified to in front of the jury. That meant that she couldn't be prosecuted for any crimes she committed.

Those words generally gave a witness great comfort, but not Dorothea. She was still struggling with the sins she committed before God. That absolution I could not give her, but I told her I was always taught that if you are sorry for your sins, God will forgive you. Apparently, those words struck a chord with her. She sat up straight in her chair, wiped the tears from her eyes, folded her hands and continued her story with Jack Keys asking questions.

A: Ms. March told me and the other morning shift lady that since Alice had trouble swallowing, she had to go on a liquid diet.
Q: Did you think she did?
A: No. She ate with the other residents in the dining room for a while after she came back from the hospital.
Q: What changed?
A: The day that Alice broke the Tiffany lamp is the day she went on the liquid diet as ordered by Ms. March.
Q: How long was Alice on the liquid diet?
A: About five months, from that day until the day she went to the hospital where she died.
Q: Did you prepare Alice's meals?

A: No. Ms. March prepared all her meals because she insisted they had to be puréed in the blender.

Q: Do you know what Alice's meals consisted of?

A: I only know that every dinner was broth. Chicken or beef. Just broth.

Q: Did you feed Alice some of her meals?

A: I would feed her dinner on the days I worked.

Q: How did Alice tolerate her liquid diet?

A: She ate all we gave her but still lost weight.

Q: Tell us about feeding Alice?

A: I would spoon-feed Alice a bowl of soup. Alice could not speak, but she could let me know she wanted more. When I told Ms. March, she said Alice was to get only one bowl of broth. When I asked if we could add some rice or noodles in the soup, she said no since Alice might choke. Alice was so sad and appeared so hungry that toward the end of June, I took a chance and would sneak a slice of bread in my pocket when I went to Alice's room to feed her. I did not want her to choke... (crying) but she looked so hungry. I would bring in the bowl of soup and then take the slice of bread out of my pocket, break it up into small pieces and put it in the soup. Alice took the soup and bread and would nod to me. This went on for about six weeks until she went to the hospital for the last time.

Q: Did you ever see Alice choke on any bread?

A: No.

Q: Did you tell Ms. March that Alice was losing weight?
A: I told her two or three times, but Ms. March said she sees Alice every day and knows her condition. She also scolded me that I was not a medical professional and that she knows what she's doing.
Q: Did you ever examine Alice's back?
A: No, only Ms. March would bathe her.

Now that we had the facts concerning Alice's treatment, the next issue was to establish the cause of her death. The Suffolk County Medical Examiner's Office was down the street from our office. The chief medical examiner was Suzanna Garteen. Dr. Suzy, as she was called, was one of the most respected pathologists in New York State. She participated in or supervised over a thousand autopsies, was on the medical advisory board of the Warren Commission investigating the Kennedy assassination and testified as an expert witness in high-profile cases throughout the state and the country.

We asked Dr. Suzy to review the hospital charts of Alice's two most recent hospitalizations and shared with her the statements made by Dorothea Halloran and Kathy Vasco. She concluded that in this case, there were three possible causes of death: (i) natural causes; (ii) advanced cancer that only could be determined by examination of the long bones of the body; (iii) homicide by starvation.

Dr. Suzy wanted to start her investigation by ruling out cancer as the cause of death. When I asked what the next step was, Keys and the doctor simultaneously responded: "You have to dig her up."

Exhuming a body is no simple task. You needed to file a detailed motion in the New York State Supreme Court seeking to convince a judge to sign an order permitting the exhumation. Once the order was signed, we had to contact the Catholic diocese of Rockville Center that operated St. Charles Cemetery to identify the grave and provide men and machines; find a local undertaker to provide a casket to rebury Alice; make arrangements with the medical examiner's office to pick up the body at the cemetery and complete a host of other small yet time-consuming tasks.

While we were working to achieve this objective, Investigator Jager wanted me to subpoena The Palace residents Atillio Del Negro, the man who spoke to Jager at the smoking parlor, and Johnny Drinkwater to testify before the grand jury. Jager was getting nowhere fast during the interviews he was conducting at The Palace as the dictatorial Ms. March insisted on being present whenever any residents or staff were interviewed.

"You are in my house, and you play by my rules or you get out" were her orders.

When we subpoenaed witnesses to the grand jury, Ms. March would not have that veto power.

Grand Jury Secrecy

A grand jury proceeding is conducted in secret, and only the grand jurors, prosecutor, grand jury reporter and witnesses are permitted in the grand jury chamber. The New York criminal procedure law provides that grand jurors are prohibited from disclosing "the nature or substance of any grand jury testimony, evidence or any decision, result or other matter, attending a grand jury proceeding." This procedure is designed to obtain the full cooperation of witnesses free from outside pressure—Ms. March in this case—and to protect an innocent person who may be investigated but never indicted.

The Alice Hightower case was moving full speed ahead and in several different directions at once, until at our weekly staff meeting, the chief investigator, Anthony Josephs, brought us back to the stark reality of the situation that seemed to get lost in the whirlwind of activity.

"For the last two weeks you guys are understandably focused on making a homicide case, but you have forgotten our true mission. While we have one former resident who may have been starved to death, we definitely have four or five elderly people tied to their beds all night every night from 7 p.m. to 7 a.m. You"—Josephs looked directly at me—"have to get your head out of your legal ass and start caring for those people who we know will be hogtied to their beds tonight. And God forbid if a fire breaks out."

Chief Josephs was clearly correct. I had lost the proverbial forest because I was looking at one tree. We did not have time to build our homicide case before we acted. We had to do something now.

Taking the chief's lead, overnight we assembled a task force of personnel from the state and county health departments to conduct a raid at The Palace.

The New York State Health Department would take the lead, and within twenty-four hours of the chief's lecture on October 16, health department investigators along with the sheriff's office arrived at The Palace with a doctor and four nurses from Stony Brook University Hospital's Geriatric Department. In the next two hours, all five residents were examined, deemed to be "medically at risk" and evacuated to the hospital by ambulance. Four of the five residents had significant—that is, stage two or stage three—decubitus ulcers. One had a stage four ulcer. Three of the five were anemic. All were dehydrated. Three of the five could not ambulate without assistance. Three of the five were suffering from infections due to their decubitus ulcers and the contamination of their wounds while they were tied in bed. Four of the five were diagnosed with muscle contractions.

The health department took photos of The Palace to document that there were no smoke detectors, fire extinguishers or an evacuation plan. The health department's preliminary conclusion was that no matter what Ms. March called The Palace, it was not a family home. The department concluded it was an unlicensed nursing home.

On the second day of his hospital stay, Atillio Del Negro got a visit from Investigator Jager, who he had previously spoken to in the "smoking parlor." This time Jager was warmly greeted by Mr. Del Negro, who was being treated for congestive heart failure in addition to the stage two decubitus ulcer on his left shoulder and the stage three bedsore on his sacrum.

Del Negro was sitting up in a recliner to lessen the pressure on his bed sores and was being given antibiotics to reduce inflammation. When Jager asked Atillio if he would cooperate in our investigation against The Palace, he responded, "First, stop calling me Atillio. Everyone calls me Pudge."

And the conversation began. Pudge prefaced his answers by saying, "I ain't no snitch, but she's got to pay for what she did to these old people."

Q: How long have you been in The Palace?
A: Call it ninety days. I got there on July 21.
Q: Who was in charge?
A: No doubt about it. It was Aurora, Aurora March.
Q: Pudge, I did a background check on you and see you were in jail several times.
A: Yeah, when I wasn't working as an exterminator,

I was part of a Gambino crew working JFK airport—usually small stuff. Then I got jammed up on a hijacking of a truck where the driver got severely hurt, and I did ten years of a fifteen-year stretch. I got out when I was seventy-five years old and retired.

Q: How did you get to The Palace?

A: My son, who is a legitimate stockbroker working downtown at the Financial District, heard of this place from some of his friends, so he asked that I move from my apartment in Howard Beach to The Palace to be close to him and the grandkids. That was bullshit because he rarely comes to see me, and the grandkids only come visit on the holidays. Guess he's ashamed to have an ex-con as a dad. Not that I was such a great dad in the first place.

Q: What was the care like at The Palace?

A: Not much better than the department of corrections, I can tell you that. There were six of us when I got there. A few weeks later, one old lady named Alice went to the hospital and never came back. Of the five of us, four could get around on our own. Only Rita Keller was wheelchair bound. The food was good but not enough. The best part was The Ladies. We called all of them The Ladies. They would cook and clean. Whenever they could, they would sit down and talk with us. We would be in the great room. Francine would be locked in on the TV, but the rest of us would be speaking to The Ladies. That was the best part of the day, someone to listen to our stories. It was hard for me because I never told anyone I was an ex-con. I made conversation leaving that out. You see, before I worked for the mob, I did some work in the Borscht Belt, the Catskills, doing standup.

Deciding What Crime to Charge

We felt we could easily charge Aurora March with third degree assault, which was a misdemeanor and carried a maximum of a year imprisonment in the Suffolk County Jail. However, the more we learned about the treatment these five individuals—and no doubt others—endured at Aurora's hands, we believed this charge to be woefully inadequate. The proper charge would be the class D felony of assault, second degree, which carried a maximum seven years in the state prison. To prove felony assault, we had to establish that Aurora March used a "dangerous instrument" to seriously injure another person. A dangerous instrument is defined as an instrument that, under the circumstances used, "was capable of causing serious physical injury, that is, physical injury creating a substantial risk of death or causes protracted disfigurement or impairment of health." It was our position that

> the Gentle Reminders constituted a dangerous instrument.
>
> It was now up to Pudge, Johnny, Francine, Rita and Stella to see if we had enough evidence to make the felony assault case.

It was Pudge who made the case with his rather graphic grand jury testimony:

Q: Do you know what a Gentle Reminder is?
A: You got to be (expletive deleted) kidding. I did two weeks in the Hole—you would call it solitary confinement—at Danamora and that was a piece of cake by comparison.
Q: How did it start?
A: When I got there the first day after I moved in and my son left, I had dinner with my new family. After dinner, Ms. March called me out to the screened-in porch and told me the rules of the house. She said that The Ladies would be with us from 7 a.m. to 7 p.m., but no one was there at night. We'd be alone just like we would be if we were in our own home. She said she was worried that if one of us got up at night to use the bathroom or go for a snack in the kitchen, we could fall, and no one would be able to assist us until the morning. So, Aurora said for our safety, we would have a Gentle Reminder to stay in our bed.

Q: Tell me what a Gentle Reminder is.
A: It's like a fancy piece of rope. One end is tied to the metal springs under the bed. The other end has a three-inch-wide cuff that gets placed over your wrist and tightened.

Q: Did you ever have a Gentle Reminder used on you?
A: Yeah, from the very first night I was there. Every night. When I asked Aurora how I could get up and use the bathroom at night, she said that would not be necessary as we would all be put in diapers at night and if we had to go ... just go.

Q: How did you react to the Gentle Reminders?
A: Not well, I guess. The very first night they put it on my left wrist and in three minutes—and I was taking my sweet time—I had it off. Bullshit! I wasn't going to go in no (expletive deleted) diaper. The next morning, The Ladies told Aurora I had removed the Gentle Reminder, and she was mad as a rattlesnake. If I didn't follow the house rules, she would tell my son and move me out and I would have no place to go. That night Aurora herself put the rope on my left wrist—and on my left ankle as well. I could undo the left wrist rope, but I couldn't bend down enough to get the leg one off.

Q: Did you have any bed sores when you came to The Palace?
A: No. They developed while I was there. Remember, you're tied to the bed so you can only lie on your back or on your left side. There's not enough length in the rope to let you turn on your right side.

Q: Did anyone else have Gentle Reminders placed on them every night?
A: Francine, Johnny and Stella. The other one, Rita, couldn't get out of bed by herself.
Q: Did you discuss the Gentle Reminders with Johnny, Stella and Francine?
A: Sure, we did. Stella and Francine accepted it, and they only had a wrist restraint on them. Johnny always took his wrist ropes off, so they put Gentle Reminders on his left wrist and right ankle. He was able to release himself from those as well, so they decided to put ankle restraints on both his hands and legs. Does Jesus on the cross mean anything to you?
Q: I am sorry to ask such a personal question, while being restrained in bed ...
A: If you're asking if we pissed or shit ourselves at night in our diapers while tied to the beds, the answer is yes. We all did, and we all hated it. Every morning when we got released, we went straight to the shower to get clean.
Q: How old were you when you lived at The Palace?
A: Eighty-six years young.

Francine, Stella and Johnny also testified in the grand jury and confirmed everything Pudge told us. Rita was too frail to testify.

Our next witness in the grand jury was Dr. Erica Freedman, chief of medicine at Stony Brook University Hospital, who testified that Pudge, Francine and Stella all had stage two and stage three decubitus ulcers on their backs. Johnny suffered contractures (a shortening and hardening of muscles and tendons leading to rigid joints) of both hips, stage four decubitus ulcers on his sacrum, a stage three on his back and stage two ulcers on the heels of both his feet. Stella had a right shoulder contracture. All four had infected bedsores because of fecal contamination and were being treated for sepsis.

Now that we had the facts established, we needed an expert physician in geriatric medicine to testify and connect the dots to establish a link between the Gentle Reminders and serious physical injury. Locating such a physician fell to Investigator Keys. I was somewhat shocked to hear from Jack that he had located a physician who graduated from Queens College to be our expert. When I expressed my concerns to Jack that although Queens College was a fine institution and part of the City University of New York system, I thought it lacked the cachet I wanted for my expert witness. Jack immediately corrected me. The physician under consideration had graduated from "the Queens College," which is part of Cambridge University in England. Doctor Cory Furlong was currently chief of the Geriatric Wellness Center at Johns Hopkins University and authored several papers on the prevention and treatment of decubitus ulcers as well as the textbook used in most medical schools. We reached out to Dr. Furlong, and after reviewing the records we had on our four alleged victims, he agreed to testify.

His conclusion was that the bed restraints called Gentle Reminders when used under these circumstances, caused serious injury to the patients and constituted a dangerous instrument.

Lastly, nurse Kathy Vasco testified concerning Alice Hightower.

After hearing all the testimony, the grand jury returned an indictment against Aurora March and The Palace Family Care Home, charging six counts of assault in the second degree, a class D felony that carries a maximum sentence of seven years in state prison. That was one count each for Pudge, Stella, Rita, Francine, Johnny, and Alice. However, the grand jury, declined to charge the crime of murder in the second degree ("death caused by evincing a depraved indifference to human life") in connection with the death of Alice Hightower. The grand jury believed we were not able to prove the cause of Alice's death was starvation.

Aurora was arrested the very day the grand jury returned the indictment and was released on bond pending trial.

The case was then assigned to Suffolk County Court Judge Terrance O'Shaughnessy, who can best be described as cranky on a good day and most times downright mean. The trial lasted for five days. Counsel for Ms. March decided that she would not testify at trial and instead presented character witnesses concerning the care provided by her at The Palace.

After all the evidence was presented, counsel for Ms. March, out of the presence of the jury, moved to dismiss all the felony charges on the grounds that the Gentle Reminders did not constitute a dangerous instrument. Judge O'Shaughnessy then called a recess to consider the motion. An hour later, the judge ruled the Gentle Reminders were, as a matter of law, a dangerous instrument.

The same argument was made to the jury by defense counsel, but to no avail. After four hours of deliberation the jury convicted Aurora March on all six counts of assault in the second degree. The judge set a sentencing date for December 21.

About a week before the sentence was to be pronounced, Ms. March's lawyer called and advised me he was going to make an application to Judge O'Shaughnessy to delay her sentence date until January 5, "so Aurora could spend the holidays at home with her family."

It was clear to all of us that a jail sentence was in her future. Counsel got the judge on a conference call and made his request for an adjournment. When he finished his application and before I could note my objection, Judge O'Shaughnessy, who himself was seventy years old, said in no uncertain terms, "I intend to show your client the same mercy she's showed those six old people each night that she had them hog-tied in bed. Motion is denied."

On December 21, 1987, Aurora March was sentenced to four years in a state prison.

On appeal, Aurora sought to have her conviction overturned on the grounds that the Gentle Reminders "were not a dangerous instrument."

The Appellate Division of the State Supreme Court heard her appeal.

Disagreed with her position.

Upheld the conviction.

CHAPTER TWO

Building the Medicaid Fraud Highway

"Have you ever been the victim of a crime?"

This is one of several questions a judge will ask you as a prospective juror. You will, most likely, respond "No, Your Honor." But you would be wrong.

You may never have faced a thug with a weapon, but you were nevertheless the victim of a crime—a theft by fraudsters who devise ingenious ways to steal your money. We are not talking about the ubiquitous telephone scams or Ponzi schemes in which you are the intended victim. Rather, I want to tell you about those criminals who perpetrate scams directed at the public at large and its vast number of faceless victims. To be more precise, you and me.

The best way to illustrate this is to share with you what I learned about two of the most interesting and costly frauds committed in recent history—healthcare fraud and automobile insurance fraud. The stories show the ingenious ways the bad guys game the system and pervert programs designed for the common good.

I learned much of what I will tell you about Medicaid fraud from investigators who were intimately involved in prosecuting these scams in the early days of the program. The stories about auto insurance fraud come from firsthand knowledge. I represented doctors against claims by various insurance companies and when those doctors were called before the New York State Board of Professional Medical Conduct, which was looking to revoke their licenses to practice. What always fascinated me is how most of these scams were started by a few people stealing small amounts of money and eventually morphed into major criminal enterprises.

Part I: Medicaid Fraud

The year was 1965. That was when the Medicare and Medicaid Act was signed into law in Washington, DC. The place was the small community of Brighton Beach situated on the Coney Island peninsula facing the Atlantic Ocean in Brooklyn, New York.

Due to the rapid immigration of Soviet nationals who left their homeland in Russia and Ukraine, Brighton was transformed into a community known as Little Odessa. As the Russian-speaking population increased, new businesses popped up, seeking to serve and to profit from the influx of immigrants. Fellow Russians opened stores that catered to the immigrant's desire for clothing, groceries and delicatessens. Not to be left out were those few who decided the way to riches in this new land was not through hard work, but rather through crime. These individuals—later dubbed the Russian mafia by law enforcement—found it easy to steal from the very trusting, and some would say very stupid, Americans. Over the next twenty-five years the Russian mob would construct a "fraud highway" originating in Brighton and spreading its tentacles throughout New York State.

What would metaphorically start as a simple country road would culminate in a superhighway where large sums of money would go from New York citizen taxpayers into the pockets of those bent on criminal conduct. The fraud highway took a degree of sophisticated planning and years to evolve, but in the end, the money, of which there was a lot, was very easy to steal. This is how it happened.

The One-Lane Road

It did not take long for the fraudsters to come up with their roadmap to steal. Many of them worked as limousine drivers. Between their pickups and drop-offs, they congregated at local delis and, with nothing but time to kill, discussed ways to supplement their income. Eventually, the word was passed around that this new program called Medicaid paid large sums for something called durable medical equipment (DME), state-speak for crutches, wheelchairs, braces and the like. It also did not take long for the businessmen to figure out that they could buy inferior DME from suppliers at a rather low cost and sell it at a higher Medicaid- approved price, pocketing the difference.

All an entrepreneur had to do was fill out an

application to become a Medicaid provider. You did not have to worry about filling out the application accurately because no one verified your statements, and since New York was so anxious to enroll as many providers as possible to start this new program, the rubber stamp of approval was all but a certainty. (Years later it would be discovered that the state of New York paid hundreds of thousands of dollars to DME providers whose address was a 40-by-100-foot empty lot filled with trash.)

The profit to be made was both significant and easy, but unfortunately for the bad guys, very erratic. To make a score, the limo-driver-turned-Medicaid-provider had to find a patient who had a doctor's order for DME and convince that patient to bring the order to the driver's newly created company. To attract patients, the driver spread word on the street that if a patient had a prescription for DME, the patient could receive $100 to $150 in cash if he used a certain driver's company.

Clearly, this hit-or-miss proposition was not sustainable in the long run. It was then that a group of the limousine drivers decided that they would join together to control all the care rendered to Medicaid patients in Brighton. To do so they would have to infiltrate and then manipulate the algorithm Medicare used to pay providers:

      Patients
    + **Doctors**
    + **Prescriptions for Ancillary Services**
       (DME, drugs, physical therapy, blood testing)
    = **Millions of Dollars**

Fraudsters are nothing if not creative. They could look at that formula, tweak it, and just like the big bang, a criminal enterprise burst into existence. Three key pillars were necessary to effectuate the Medicaid scam:

✦ Enroll patients into the Medicaid program.
✦ Find cooperating physicians who would treat patients and, more importantly, write prescriptions for medically unnecessary ancillary services.
✦ Set up a network of ancillary service providers willing to pay kickbacks to capture every nickel of Medicaid dollars Brighton could generate.

With those goals established, the fledgling Russian mob started to put its plan into action.

Mafia soldiers, masquerading as businessmen, would meet newly arriving immigrants and extol all the benefits that the American government provides, especially healthcare. The individuals targeted were predominately the elderly or unemployed who jumped at the opportunity to see a doctor—and for free.

Teams of businessmen would take vanloads of immigrants to the local social services office to be enrolled. Once an individual officially became a Medicaid recipient they would be shown "appreciation," as was the custom in the USSR. That meant the businessman would place a crisp twenty-dollar bill in their hand with the promise of more appreciation—if they did what they were told.

The second step of the scam was to find a group of physicians who would work with the businessmen—and it turned out to be easier than originally anticipated.

Once again, the mob preyed on the weak. Physicians who were trained to practice medicine in a foreign country could not be licensed in the United States until 1971, when the magnanimous American Medical Association developed the Fifth Pathway. This allowed certain students who graduated from foreign medical schools to complete their supervised clinical training in the United States, apply for US residency programs and ultimately obtain a license.

Many of the Fifth Pathway practitioners were discriminated against by other physicians, who regarded them as second-class doctors who were not smart enough to be accepted into an American medical school.

Hence, most Fifth Pathway doctors wound up practicing at local community hospitals like Coney Island Hospital in Brighton. They worked as emergency room physicians or took night call for other physicians or struggled as solo practitioners in a community that could not pay the usual medical fees the American doctors charged. The one thing all these physicians had in common was that they worked long hours for very little compensation and were angry at the system that seemed rigged against them. These downtrodden physicians became easy targets of the mob because they held the key to the second part of the scam: a medical license.

The next step was to infiltrate ancillary medical providers in the community. In the mid-1970s, almost anyone who did not have a criminal record could become a Medicaid provider of ancillary medical services. It was easy for physicians to enroll as owners of blood testing labs or physical therapy practices while nonlicensed individuals could provide such things as wheelchairs, oxygen tanks, pressure mattresses or other equipment that Medicaid deemed a therapeutic benefit to a patient.

A typical scenario consisted of a group of newly enrolled Medicaid recipients being shepherded in a van for a ride to a doctor's office. It was called a clinic, and it was controlled by the mob. To show their appreciation to the patient, the clinic's manager would dole out the traditional twenty-dollar bill. Once the new patient arrived at the clinic, the co-opted doctor would provide a cursory exam lasting a few minutes and then bill Medicaid for the higher reimbursed, comprehensive medical exam, which typically took forty-five to sixty minutes.

The doctor would keep 30 percent of the reimbursement from Medicaid with the balance going to a mob associate who controlled the patients. The doctors were ecstatic with this deal. They were getting paid for significantly more patients' visits than they would without the mob's help.

In return, the doctor was ordered to write prescriptions for expensive medications, physical therapy services, lab tests and an array of other services. If the doctor did not, the mob would cease working with him, or worse things could happen. The patient also benefited by being shown additional appreciation if he and his newly written prescriptions went to a mob-controlled provider.

The pharmacies, blood labs and DME equipment providers were also told they had to kick back a substantial portion of their Medicaid payments to the businessman or else they would never see another Medicaid patient. To pay the kickback and still make the profit they wanted, these providers began to bill for services they did not render or bill for high-priced services when inferior services were actually provided. All this was done to steal Medicaid dollars, and the perpetrators never felt a pang of guilt as the working diagnosis was: after all, *these people aren't sick anyway*.

In the fifteen years between the creation of the Medicaid program and the establishment of the New York State Attorney General's Medicaid Fraud Control Unit (MFCU) in 1975, the Brighton area of Brooklyn became the Dodge City of healthcare fraud. Lawlessness abounded, and there was no sheriff to protect the citizens. The MFCU became that sheriff, and I was privileged to join that office in the middle of 1976. With the power to audit, investigate and prosecute criminal conduct in the Medicaid arena, we had a slew of targets to investigate with only a small task force. As we dug in, the greed of the mobsters and Medicaid providers led to some bizarre cases. Here are some examples.

Ultraviolet Cabinets

Perhaps one of the most bizarre products billed to Medicaid was the ultraviolet cabinet. Ultraviolet cabinets were used to alleviate intractable psoriasis, a condition that purportedly grew to epidemic proportions in the elderly Brighton community.

Maybe the real reason for that epidemic was the price of the cabinet. It was one of the most expensive pieces of DME equipment on the Medicaid list.

This piece of DME was as big as a telephone booth and was fitted with high-intensity ultraviolet lights. The patient was to stand in this cabinet for several minutes each day to cure psoriasis that could not be cured by any other treatment modality, as attested to by the patient's doctor.

You could imagine the shock on the face of an elderly patient who had a six-foot by two-foot cabinet brought into her small Brooklyn apartment to cure a disease that she did not have. Not only would she reject the delivery, she'd curse out the driver in her native tongue.

Uproars like this eventually caused the unscrupulous DME providers to submit a bill to Medicaid but not deliver any product. Other DME providers chose to deliver a wooden box measuring six inches by six inches with one UVA bulb, claiming it was an ultraviolet cabinet and billing Medicaid $4,000.

Physical Therapists

Mobsters liked working with physical therapists because patients became a sort of annuity. They would be seen two or three times a week for at least six weeks. The billing would start with a patient evaluation that could range from a level of "low complexity" to one of "high complexity." And yes, you guessed it, most of the billings were for high complexity patient evaluations.

Therapeutic procedures could be billed in increments of fifteen minutes, but no matter how much time a patient was treated, a bill for an hour of physical therapy was submitted.

Initially, it was easy to get patients to go to a physical therapist because the patient was shown appreciation to the tune of fifty dollars instead of the usual twenty. However, patients often got tired of receiving weeks of physical therapy for an ailment they really did not have.

To counter this reluctance, the businessmen hired motivators to ensure the patients complied with their doctor's orders. One such person was Gregori Zlotnich. He stood six feet five and weighed about four hundred pounds. His nickname Globus, meaning world, said it all. In his conversation with a reluctant patient, Globus would remind the patient of his previous commitment and would explain that if he failed to continue to receive medical treatment, Globus himself would ensure the patient sustained real physical injuries that would require a trip to

Coney Island Hospital's emergency room followed by, no doubt, extensive physical therapy.

After this motivational talk, the patient almost always completed the prescribed course of physical therapy.

Blood Testing Labs

Every patient who went to a clinic owned by the mob left with an order for a blood test. Since most elderly patients did not wish to go to a lab and have a needle inserted into their arm by a technician who may or may not have received training as a phlebotomist, the clinic would provide the lab with just the patient's name and Medicaid number. No blood. This allowed the lab to produce a bogus lab report but a very real bill to Medicaid.

Some labs also treated patients with commercial health insurance. They would purchase an expensive automated blood-testing machine called a Sequential Multiple Analysis Computer (SMAC) that would run a twenty-test panel on a single sample of blood, thus increasing the amounts that could be billed. A few labs were so confident that the fledgling Medicaid program did not have the capability to audit their claims, they had the cojones to bill Medicaid for a SMAC panel even though they did not even own the machine.

Prior to the mob getting involved in the Medicaid program, the practice of medicine was based on the honor system. Doctors ordered lab tests to assist them in evaluating a patient. The lab diligently ran the tests and provided the results to the physician, who relied on them to arrive at a diagnosis and treatment plan. The mob perverted this concept into one where the main concern was billing, not patient care. The doctors who ordered lab tests they knew to be of little or no diagnostic use and the labs who provided falsified blood tests all bought into the mob's philosophy that it did not matter if the tests were performed or not. The rationale once again: *these patients are not really sick.*

After many years passed, Medicaid started to conduct a basic audit of the program. Immediately, the auditors found the number of blood tests being billed in the Brighton community was significantly higher than in similar communities and was skyrocketing. Word spread on the street that Medicaid and state health inspectors would soon be assigned to check lab equipment and verify their test results.

This posed a problem for the mob's labs because they did not have backup for the tests they performed. The mob had to counter Medicaid's anticipated move. They realized the importance of a paper trail to justify the blood tests they billed, or they would be denied payment. Or perhaps the ultimate sanction would be imposed: the revocation of their Medicaid provider number.

Since more and more of the elderly Brighton residents refused to have blood drawn no matter how much the appreciation was, the mob had to come up with another plan to justify their Medicaid billings.

One plan they devised required the use of drug addicts, an apartment on the Lower West Side of Manhattan, a kitchen table, plastic bags, tubing and a needle. A simple, inexpensive plan, but it would lead to big problems for the mob.

Early one morning in October 1976, a thirty-year-old male was found unresponsive on the sidewalk at Tenth Avenue and Twenty-Third Street and was taken by ambulance to Beekman Downtown Hospital. The patient looked thin and pale, was cold to the touch and had the appearance of a drug addict, confirmed by the track marks on both arms. However, he did not exhibit the traditional symptoms of a drug overdose. The patient's blood pressure was dangerously low; he had a rapid heartbeat, shallow breathing and continued to be unresponsive to stimuli. After a quick evaluation by the emergency room's chief resident, Dr. Simon Goldberg, the diagnosis was that the patient was bleeding to death.

Because there was no outward sign of trauma, the bleeding had to be internal. Dr. Goldberg was convinced that if he did not find and seal off the cause of the internal bleeding the patient would surely die. A second transfusion was given, and Dr. Shelly Wang, a trauma surgeon, was called. As the trauma team prepared for an exploratory examination of the patient's abdomen, a third transfusion was given along with additional fluids.

The patient was on the operating room table and Dr. Wang was in the process of performing her usual patient exam prior to commencing surgery when the man appeared to respond. Dr. Wang delayed surgery and ordered additional tests. To everyone's surprise, the more sophisticated tests indicated there was no active bleeding.

The surgeon and chief resident had seen many traumas during their five years at Beekman, but this case did not fit any of those scenarios. Nevertheless, trusting her gut, she canceled the surgical procedure and ordered another pint of blood.

Slowly the young man started to come around while the fourth pint of blood coursed through his veins.

The story the patient told the doctors that morning led to a search warrant being executed at the residence located on Twenty-First Street by the New York City Emergency Services Division. The search warrant uncovered facts that confirmed the story told by the young patient. He had gone to that location based upon information he got from other addicts. The deal was simple—he would go to that apartment, be paid thirty dollars and have a pint of blood removed from his veins. Prior to being placed on the table in the apartment's kitchen, he was given a medication that made him feel lightheaded. Blood was drawn; he was given the thirty dollars and sent on his way. He barely walked two blocks before he passed out on the concrete.

Beekman's medical staff concluded the patient was suffering from hypovolemic shock—a life threating condition—since five pints of blood (half of a person's blood volume) was taken from the man. This conclusion was corroborated by occupants of the apartment who were told that they would be charged with attempted murder if they failed to cooperate with the authorities. Those arrested quickly gave up two individuals in Brighton who agreed to pay them fifty dollars for every pint of blood they were able to deliver. No questions asked.

When this pattern of criminality—not to mention indifference to human suffering—came to light, the MFCU and the NYPD formed a partnership to go after the mobsters. We called the taskforce Operation Vampire. Three other blood drawing sites were discovered and raided.

As in the initial case, when those arrested understood that they were facing charges of felony assault, attempted murder or conspiracy to commit murder if one of the victims died, they decided to cooperate with the investigation and give us the people for whom they were working. Once the mob understood the investigators of Operation Vampire were able to identify the locations of the illegal blood drawing operations, they quickly shut them down.

Although only running for a short time, Vampire was considered a success because we stopped not only a fraud but ended a practice that placed the lives of victims at significant risk.

As a sidenote, the mobsters also made it easy for us to spot fraudulent billing for blood testing; when the test results for the billing were audited, it revealed the identical blood values for hundreds of patients billed to the program, providing concrete evidence of fraud.

The Two-Lane Boulevard

As time passed, the freelance mobster businessmen started to grow into a true organized syndicate. To generate more and more money, the mob sought to expand their criminal enterprise beyond using elderly immigrants as their pawns to steal from Medicaid. They selected as their next victims the people who were more vulnerable than the elderly and for whom they did not have to show appreciation—drug addicts.

Doctors remained the linchpin for the fraud's success, but this time the mobsters sought to target heroin addicts by giving them an easier and cheaper way to get high—prescription opioid drugs.

The addict community soon found out that if you were on Medicaid and went to the office of a certain doctor you would get a script for a narcotic drug and your only payment would be your Medicaid card. Once the doctor had the addict's Medicaid billing information, it allowed the doctor to bill not only for a bogus visit but for a host of diagnostic tests that were never performed. The addict would not complain as long as they got a prescription for a thirty-day supply of a narcotic drug, which of course would be filled at a mob-controlled pharmacy. The pharmacy would bill

Medicaid for the narcotics and give the pills to its customer, usually shorting the number of pills dispensed. The profit on the doctor visits and prescriptions was then split with the mobsters. In thirty days, the entire cycle would be repeated, guaranteeing an annuity for the thieves and a source of drugs for the addict. Truly, a win-win situation. But, of course, nothing lasts forever, especially when greed sets in.

As time passed, the addicts became more and more belligerent, demanding higher potency medication and a larger supply of pills, to the point of threatening physicians with physical violence. The tension between the doctor and his patient grew so strong that several doctor's offices, known as pill mills—catering solely to the addicts from Brighton and surrounding areas—sought to protect themselves. The protection took the form of a fortified medical office. In this type of office, the patient would approach the physician's receptionist who sat in a bulletproof glass enclosure and produce a Medicaid card. The employee would verify the patient's Medicaid eligibility, then disappear into a back room and return with a prescription for narcotic drugs, which were passed through a metal slot such as was used in a bank. "Visit over. See you next month."

Only rarely was a physician seen in the office, but one or two mob enforcers were clearly visible in the waiting room to ensure order.

CASES YOU CAN'T MAKE UP

⁕ The Four-Lane Parkway ⁕

Over the years, the addict population served by the mobsters became more and more unruly. To avoid dealing with them, the mob shifted their patient profile to a more docile clientele. In 1981, the New York City area was dramatically impacted by the AIDS epidemic and went on to have the unfortunate distinction of having more AIDS cases than any city in the world. Treatments were fast-tracked to fight the epidemic, and in 1987, Burroughs Wellcome introduced the first drug to treat AIDS known as Retrovir, more commonly called AZT. It was estimated that over 35 percent of New York City's AIDS patients lacked any type of health insurance. Medicaid became the chief source of payment for their AZT. The cost: $8,000 to $10,000 per person per month.

Not wanting to miss out on an opportunity to profit from another human being's misfortune, the mob, now formally known as the Russian mafia, developed two new strategies. First, they placed a bounty on each AIDS patient delivered to one of their clinics. Second, the mob was getting tired of making the doctors rich in the scams they devised, developed and financed. So, they took the next step in building the fraud highway. The mob told the Fifth Pathway doctors who were already in their pockets that they now worked for them and were on a salary. The profits of the medical practice would now go directly to the mob. If the doctor refused, he could make a choice. He could go to work at a hospital or set up his own private practice where the mob would make sure he would never see a Medicaid patient. Many of the recruited doctors were used to living the good life, and they reluctantly agreed to the new terms that were dictated to them.

To jump-start their new initiative using AIDS patients, the Mob created a new job title, that of runner. The runner's job would be to haunt soup kitchens, flophouses and homeless shelters looking for AIDS patients. Once identified, the patients would be directed to a specific doctor's office, and in return the runner would get paid a hundred-dollar cash bounty for each patient delivered. There existed no cure for AIDS. A visit to the doctor's office consisted of a brief exam, if a medical exam was performed at all. The sole purpose of the visit was to justify a script for ATZ.

As more and more AIDS patients entered the mob-run healthcare system, some doctors and pharmacists really wanted to help this patient population, which now included their friends and family members. The old line used to rationalize their overbilling and lack of medical care for elderly patients—these people are not really sick—clearly did not apply. To counter this sentiment among some of its workers, the mob rebranded its mantra and insisted that the current procedure of running patients through the medical clinics without really providing medical care, should continue because: *these people are going to die anyway.*

However, before the AIDS patients went to greet their Maker, they had to be used to line the pockets of the unscrupulous.

The mob would send all the AIDS patients they purchased from their runners to their doctor, and then their blood lab (you can bet no blood from the AIDS victim was actually drawn because everyone knew the deadly virus was transmitted by bodily fluids) and then to their crown jewel— the pharmacy.

Faced with a death sentence, many AIDS patients were easily manipulated by the mob pharmacies who cared more for money than human suffering,

Many pharmacy managers made an offer: "Hey, if you don't want your AZT, give me the script and help yourself to a hundred dollars' worth of merchandise in the store."

Sadly, many infected with AIDS who had seen their friends die a miserable death on the streets opted for immediate gratification of soap, shampoo, combs, cigarettes and most of all candy. A hundred dollars was a small price to pay to bill Medicaid $9,000 for the AZT that the pharmacy did not need to buy and, of course, never distributed, thus making pure profit.

Eventually, audits by the New York State Department of Health and Medicaid Fraud Control Unit would show Medicaid was billed for tens of thousands of AZT pills, while the pharmacies would be lucky to show purchases in the hundreds. Over several years, pharmacy owners, pharmacists and doctors, as well as a few mobsters, were indicted. A significant amount of money was recouped, some of the indicted were sentenced to jail, and some would lose their license to practice. But this was just the tip of the lengths the mob would go to fill their coffers with illegal gains.

It Never Stops

The story I just told you wrapped up the late 1990s. While it was the end for those who participated in this particular fraud, it is not the end of the story. Rather, it is the first in a long line of fraud cases that target you and me by diverting our tax dollars into the pocket of thieves wearing the disguises of doctor, pharmacist, businessman—but thieves nevertheless.

Medicaid fraud (as well as thefts from the Medicare program) continues to this day and is probably occurring as you read this. As recently as October 2023, the United States attorney for the Southern District of New York indicted nine people in a twenty-million-dollar fraud in which these individuals "paid patients to sell back their HIV meds" to a pharmacy that then sold them on the black market to other pharmacies "around the country" for resale. Once again, the HIV patient was exploited, and the bad guys profited. According to the United States Attorney's Office, "The defendants spent the

> *proceeds of the scheme to purchase luxury cars, including a 2021 Mercedes-Benz Maybach, the model reputed to be the purest interpretation of sophistication and luxury, with an estimated fair market value of $245,000; waterfront real estate, including two properties in the Bronx purchased for total of $2.4 million; designer clothes; and jewelry and gold."*
>
> So, if you were ever asked the question, "Have you ever been the victim of a crime?" you now know to answer affirmatively.

Part II: Automobile Insurance Fraud

The Six-Lane Expressway

As you've seen, the mob and its frauds evolve with the times. When New York changed its automobile insurance laws in 1971, the mob pounced, and eventually I got involved.

Prior to 1971, the damages caused by a car accident were paid by the individual (in reality, that person's insurance company) who was "at fault" in the accident. Clearly, the adjudication of who was at fault and to what degree could lead to much litigation.

New York's new No-Fault Law was intended to ensure that insurance carriers would pay for "legitimate and related medical expenses, loss of earnings and incidental costs," of the people it insured without regard as to who was at fault in an accident. The legislature believed that this change in law would save expensive and extensive litigation costs and thus work to the benefit of the insurance carriers as well as the citizens whose premiums would be lower.

The passage of the No-Fault Law was a windfall for the mob. Previously, they had one insurance provider to defraud, and that was Medicaid. Now they could defraud all insurance carriers who wrote auto accident policies in New York.

Mob to Organized Crime

While I prosecuted and later defended people charged with Medicaid fraud, the individuals I met in the no-fault insurance scam were a much different breed. Medicaid fraudsters were opportunists working in individual neighborhoods. These fraudsters generally had real jobs and stealing was their side hustle. The no-fault group on the other hand went beyond their neighborhoods, and their sole occupation was to steal. They created a hierarchy—similar to the boss, capo, soldiers and associates of the Italian mafia—to conduct their business. They pulled in other people they needed,

> *especially physicians, with the hope and offer of getting rich quickly for doing very little work. However, once these individuals were hooked, the Russian mafia obtained what they wanted through fear and intimidation.*
>
> *I saw this firsthand when I represented doctors and others who had fallen for offers of lucrative employment. No matter how you judge these doctors, once caught in the mob's web, they could never get out.*

Just as in Medicaid fraud, the first piece of the scam was the creation of a "medical clinic." In New York, only a licensed medical doctor could own a medical practice, so the mob created a structure where a physician—the owner-physician—would open a medical professional corporation, (the PC), and the PC would employ a working physician who was told by the mob which medical services to provide.

Mob-selected patients were referred to these doctors, and the doctor's PC billed the insurance companies.

The first step in the no-fault scam involved a mob soldier approaching a local physician, often one who participated in the Fifth Pathway and who was just getting financially by, with a job offer. When the nice mobster visited Dr. Yuri, the conversation went something like this:

"Dr. Yuri, we will set you up in a medical practice. It will be called the Potemkin Medical Clinic. We will pay all your employee expenses, rent and taxes. We will send our patients to your clinic, and you just have to see the patients and send them where we tell you for testing and other medical supplies. We then deposit all the money generated by the clinic into a bank account that we set up for you. You give us signatory power over the account. We handle everything.

"In return, we pay you $175,000 per year. Let me say that again, Dr. Yuri—$175,000 per year for working only twenty to twenty-five hours a week."

It was truly an offer too good to refuse and was accepted readily by Dr. Yuri as well as other selected physicians in the Brighton community. What the doctors failed to realize was they had just sold their professional souls to the Russian mob.

Now that the mob had its "working doctor" in place, they needed a front who would act as the owner of the medical professional corporation (PC) as only a licensed medical doctor could incorporate such an entity

'I Know Nothing!'

One such physician, Sinha Patel, owned more than 10 PCs in one Brooklyn neighborhood alone. Dr. Patel was paid a fee by the mob to incorporate the PC and sign the PC stock certificate in blank which allowed the mob to sell the PC to anyone they wished at any time they wished. For his trouble, Doctor Patel was paid $5,000 for each PC he formed. Further investigations revealed that Dr. Patel did not know how many PCs he owned, their names, the locations, the names of the physician hired, how much profit each office made or whether any state or federal income tax returns were filed.

Now that the mob had its clinic and a physician to work there, the next task was to establish a protocol for each accident patient who came through the clinic's door. Specifically, each patient would be given a full and complete physical examination —at least on paper— as well as a full battery of diagnostic tests, such as neurological tests and x-rays.

The office manager provided by the mob directed the doctor that no matter what the examination revealed, every patient was to get an order for six weeks of physical therapy and be sent to a physical therapy practice owned by the mob. The doctor was also told to order a Magnetic Resonance Imaging (MRI) scan of the injured patient and direct the patient to a radiology practice in the area that was paying a kickback to the mob. Lastly, the doctor would be told how to write his medical evaluation of the patient to establish medical necessity for the tests he ordered both at the clinic and the other ancillary providers. This would ensure payment from a no-fault insurance carrier.

Once the clinic was created and protocols established, the issue of getting accident victims to attend the clinic needed to be addressed. The first order of business was to find patients who were not seriously injured. The clinic was looking for patients who were, in fact, in an automobile accident but not seriously injured except for the usual bumps and bruises one would suffer in any automobile collision. The goal was to miraculously transform a bumps and bruises case into one that would justify the slew of tests and fees for the clinic. Hence, a new mob mantra was created for these clinics: It doesn't matter what we do for the patient because *these people aren't really hurt anyway.*

The mob once again relied on the tried-and-true runner system to get the names of auto accident victims who went to a hospital emergency room and were treated and released. Once a name was obtained, the clinic would send out its manager to convince the individual that they should seek outpatient medical treatment. The manager had already given the runner a hundred dollars. It was now his job to close the deal with the patient. He had two ways to meet his goal. One, the patient would be told that he could make $500 in cash if he went to the specified clinic for examinations and tests, attend physical therapy for six weeks and submit to an MRI examination. Two, the patient would be conned into undergoing extensive testing and rehabilitation by being told it was necessary in order to build up his damages for a personal injury lawsuit, which could be extremely lucrative.

MRI scans were another gold mine for the clinic. An MRI scanner costs more than $400,000. The mob did not want to make such a sizable investment; rather, they decided to send their patients to local radiology practices that had an understanding with the mobsters. Pursuant to this understanding, every patient sent to the radiologist earned the mafia a kickback of $250 per scan initially, later increasing to $750 per scan, and most patients had three scans ordered for the cervical, thoracic and lumbar spine. The radiology practice had no problem paying the kickback, because at that time each MRI scan could be billed to the insurance carriers in the amount of $3,000.

To justify this billing to the insurance company and ensure payment, the radiologist had to find a medical necessity to justify an MRI scan. Accordingly, every patient was found to have spinal injuries. Because payment of the kickback to the mob guaranteed patient referrals, the radiology practices became sloppy.

In one case investigators reported that a certain radiologist would read MRI scans while he sat in a traffic jam at the Holland Tunnel on his way home to New Jersey.

No one really cared because everyone involved bought into the mob mantra that these people aren't really hurt.

After gaining some experience, the mob became concerned that the use of runners and lawyers looking to bring no-fault lawsuits for personal injury cases was not producing enough patients needed to generate the profit they were anticipating. Clearly, accident victims did not grow on trees … or did they?

Soon they realized they could produce their own accident victims. Brooklyn's Belt Parkway was nearby and convenient.

The new method for securing these patients was much like making a Bolognese sauce for your pasta. The recipe was simple:

◆ Go across the Hudson River to the New Jersey used-car auction, and buy a modest, nondescript, medium-size vehicle.
◆ Bring the car back to New York, and get it insured by a selected insurance company deemed to be a good payer.
◆ Get the car registered in New York, and do not use it for four to six weeks.
◆ Remove the lenses from the car's backup lights,

and partially unscrew the lightbulbs so they do not work but keep the bulbs in their sockets. Reinstall the lenses.
+ Load your car with four other individuals who were recruited by or worked for the mob in low-level capacities.
+ Take the car and its passengers down Coney Island Avenue, and get on the Belt Parkway.
+ Drive around until you see an expensive car such as a BMW, Mercedes, Lincoln or Cadillac.
+ Get in front of said expensive car.
+ Hit your breaks hard. Your brake lights won't go on and ... crash!

And you now have five new no-fault patients for your medical office.

This was clearly a dangerous activity to engage in, but everyone was on board because it was a moneymaker. After the first several accidents, even the bad guys came to the realization that since you could not anticipate the actions of the innocent driver, sometimes people really did get hurt. This situation had to be corrected because none of the medical professionals being used to perpetrate this scam really wanted—or frankly were competent—to treat people who were truly injured in a motor vehicle accident. To cut down on this danger factor, the recipe needed to be adjusted.

The change involved the purchasing of two cars at the New Jersey auction and getting both insured and registered in New York. Each car was still packed with three or four passengers, but this time, instead of cruising the Belt Parkway, the drivers agreed to meet at a designated intersection and at a designated time to have a designated accident. This new procedure gave the drivers control of the degree of force with which one car would strike the other. It was designed to cut down on real injuries while making the fake injuries look good.

Heard It on Tape

By 1994, I worked as a defense attorney in private practice. My client, John, was a six-foot, 275-pound limousine driver, originally from the town of Odessa in the Ukraine, who dabbled in Medicaid fraud. Somehow, he got involved with a ring that stole luxury cars and sold them to chop shops for parts. This led to John being arrested by detectives of the Brooklyn Rackets Bureau. John had a prior felony conviction, so if he was convicted of the current charge, he would be facing a mandatory prison sentence. Being the sole financial supporter of his family of six, John was looking for a deal. Unfortunately, the prosecutor assigned to John's case was the very opinionated—and I thought unreasonable— assistant chief of the Rackets Bureau, Doug

Maury. Doug and I had two previous run-ins, and we did not like each other. When I got a call from Doug requesting a meeting with John and me, I was surprised. I was more surprised when Doug said the meeting would take place at a nondescript office located on Schermerhorn Street in downtown Brooklyn instead of the district attorney's office. When I asked for some clarification, all Doug would say was, "Do you want to meet or not?"

This request was so intriguing, I had to accept the invitation. The meeting was held in the basement office of the building's superintendent. A kid who looked to be in his late teens or early twenties opened the door and led John and me to a barren office furnished with a metal desk and four folding chairs.

After a cold greeting from Doug, we were invited to take our seats. Doug said to me, "Since neither or us speak Russian, why don't you and I sit back while John and Officer Anatoly Federson"—pointing to the kid—"have an off-the-record discussion."

The back-and-forth of the conversation lasted twenty to twenty-five minutes until John stood up, as did Federson. They shook hands as John said, "Da, ya sdelayu, u tebya yest sdelka," Translated: "Yes, I will. You have a deal."

With those words, the case against John would be dismissed on the condition he introduce Grischa—Officer Federson—to three individuals the police believed to be heavily involved in the no-fault auto insurance ring.

John did so, and after several meetings, Grischa was present at the following conversation, which was duly recorded on a body recorder that he wore.

Vasily: We need more patients for our clinic, and you have been asked to participate in this task. How many cars do we have registered and ready to go?

Sasha: We have a total of eight vehicles. Only three of them have been registered and insured for more than thirty days. We wait thirty days before we use a car, so it doesn't look like the car was purchased solely to be used in an accident.

Yegor: I have ten people lined up as passengers. I would like to use the older ones as they are more likely to go through the medical testing.

Vasily: Fine. On this coming Wednesday, Sasha, you take three people and meet Yegor in a car with four people at the corner of Neptune Avenue and Brighton Fifth at 12:30.

> **Sasha:** I can't make it Wednesday at 12:30. How about we do it Friday at 10:30?
> **Yegor:** 10:30 is no good for me. How about 1:30?
> **Sasha:** Friday at 1:30 is fine at the place mentioned.
> **Vasily:** Then it's done.
>
> Just as you would meet with the friend to set up a lunch date, the bad guys would meet to set up a phony accident.
>
> There were three additional outcomes to the meeting. Federson was such a good undercover officer, he not only learned of drug and illegal gun sales, after six months he was also invited to become an associate in the mob. John had his case dismissed and left New York. Doug and I became friends, and fourteen years later we were partners in the white-collar-crime defense team at my law firm.

When phony accidents proved too complicated or difficult to set up, the mob's plan again evolved. Now, you would take a car duly insured and registered in New York to an underpass just off the Belt Parkway. To cut down on the possibility that someone might accidentally get hurt, even in a staged accident, a car was set up with its engine running twenty feet from an underpass abutment. With the use of a broom handle, the gas pedal was depressed, and the car crashed into the cement barricade. The car was then driven or pushed onto the side of the highway, and four of your friends would run to the car. The driver would then call the police and claim he was involved in a hit-and-run accident ... and more importantly, all his passengers were injured but not sufficiently to go to the hospital. Rather, the injured patients would go to a medical clinic to get checked out.

Eventually, the insurance carriers realized that the phony accidents scam was costing them millions of dollars in fraudulent claims. While their complaints to law enforcement took time to be investigated, several of the larger no-fault carriers had had enough and decided to take matters into their own hands. They went on the offensive.

The carriers shut off the spigot and stopped paying suspicious claims.

Just like that, the mob's clinics were reeling from the sudden loss of income. Before they could react, the carriers landed their second punch by suing the clinics and the doctors who supposedly owned them personally for the full amount of the claims already paid, alleging fraud.

The allegation of fraud took many forms, including alleging the clinics were really owned not by a medical professional but by businesspeople not entitled to bill for health care services.

Their third punch landed at the heart of the scam by filing complaints with the Office of Professional Medical Conduct, seeking revocation of the doctor's

CASES YOU CAN'T MAKE UP

licenses. Hence, practically overnight, a doctor who on paper owned a clinic but in truth was merely a paid employee found himself named as a defendant in a lawsuit and personally facing a judgment in the millions of dollars as well as a proceeding seeking to revoke his medical license.

―――◆―――

In 2001, I represented one such doctor who sold her medical license to the mob, which in turn established a clinic in her name. An insurance company filed a lawsuit against the clinic and more importantly against the doctor, seeking 1.4 million dollars in damages for fraudulent billing. Even more disastrous for my client, the carrier threatened to file a complaint with the New York State Department of Health seeking to revoke her license on the grounds of fraudulent conduct.

Doctor Viktoriya Lebedev was thirty-five years old and had two children, ages two and five. Her husband worked as a waiter at Rasputin, an upscale restaurant in the heart of Brighton. Viktoriya, a Fifth Pathway physician, was relegated to working the 11 p.m. to 7 a.m. shift at Coney Island Hospital's emergency room, covering for other scheduled physicians, who then would pay her part of their shift salary. Her goal was to move her family out of its small two-bedroom apartment, and when a clinic manager approached her with the "Dr. Yuri deal" she jumped at it. All Viktoriya had to do to go home with an excellent salary was to sign some papers opening a bank account and work in an office Monday through Thursday 9 a.m. to 3 p.m. While on paper she was the owner, she actually was no more than an employee and knew nothing of the office is billing or referral practices.

Now, with a pending 1.4-million-dollar lawsuit against her personally and the threat of having her license revoked, she reached out to me.

After months of intense negotiations, the insurance company agreed to withdraw their suit and not file a complaint with the department of health if the doctor agreed to walk away from $300,000 of pending medical claims "her" clinic had billed. I thought it was an excellent resolution of the lawsuit from the doctor's perspective, but I was unable to contact her at her office or on her cell phone.

Eventually, I reached Viktoriya's husband at their home and started to discuss the resolution of the case with him. His response was short and forceful. First, I was fired from representing the doctor, and second, she would not speak to me.

When I insisted on speaking to her, the husband informed me that Viktoriya and their two toddlers were leaving New York that very night for an undisclosed location. When I attempted to get more information concerning her decision, the husband cut me off. "It's because of you. Last night we got a visit by two very large individuals who said they represented the clinic owners. They told us that if Viktoriya renounced the pending claims with the insurance carrier, she and her entire family would die. To make sure we got the message, they told us that her car, the blue Ford Explorer she purchased only three weeks ago, which was stolen this morning, could be found in the Jersey Meadowlands. However, her shiny new blue car was now a burnt-out hulk of sheet metal."

The conversation concluded with Viktoriya's husband thanking me for my efforts on their behalf. He also passed on to me the fact that their late-night visitors also suggested that lawyers like me should stop meddling in the business affairs of Russian doctors as it could be "unhealthy." I guessed that was a hint.

After that conversation, I never heard from or about Viktoriya or her family again, and fortunately I never heard from her visitors either.

As a result of the carriers' action on the civil front and the vigorous prosecution of insurance fraud by the Kings County District Attorney's Office, the rash of phony accidents came to an end. The phony accidents scam had continued for more than five years and household-name insurance companies were ripped off for millions of dollars. And again, you and I, honest people who needed to buy automobile insurance, became the victims of the crime because the carriers had to raise premium rates to compensate for the false claims they paid out.

This fraud highway was shut down, but recently newer, larger and more sophisticated super freeways are being constructed.

Point in fact, on June 20, 2024, the United States Attorney for the Southern District of New York announced that leaders of one of the largest no-fault frauds in New York history were sentenced to fifteen, twelve, and seven years in federal prison.

For seven years, three individuals organized and operated a criminal enterprise that stole over forty million dollars from no-fault insurance companies. They used some of the methods I have described but on a larger scale. They bribed physicians to prescribe unnecessary medical tests and order unnecessary medical equipment. They bribed hospital employees, 911 dispatchers and even a New York City police officer to obtain confidential information concerning accident victims. Foreign nationals who came to the United States on visitor's visas were paid to open bank accounts in the name of shell corporations.

They even co-opted a law firm to launder their illegal gains by paying purported legal fees, when the money was in fact used to purchase real estate for the thieves.

These three individuals, who used stolen money to pay for luxury vacations around the world, expensive meals, jewelry, parties, and construction of a multi-million-dollar home in Queens, now had the opportunity to experience the accommodations provided by the Federal Bureau of Prisons.

Guess some people never learn.

CHAPTER THREE

Cases from a Defense Attorney's Files

In 1988, I became a defense attorney. If I thought it would have been impossible to make up the stuff I had seen as a prosecutor, well, just wait.

Does an MRI Exam Hurt?

I was attending a neighborhood barbecue on the Saturday before Labor Day 1993 and my pager went off. It was 4:14 p.m. I did not recognize the number that appeared, but I knew the meaning of the attached message, DEFCON 1.

DEFCON is the military term for Defense Readiness Condition, describing the graduated levels of military readiness. DEFCON 5 indicates normal peacetime readiness, DEFCON 1 means the world is on fire. The country went to DEFCON 3 on September 11, 2001. Only once in our nation's history was the level raised to DEFCON 2, and that was during the Cuban missile crisis in October 1962. This call was the highest alert—the prelude to war. I got to a phone and returned the call. It came from the office of Dr. Calliope Pagonis, formerly Colonel Calliope Pagonis, United States Marine Corps. She had retired to the private practice of medicine.

"Callie, it's Gregg. What happened?"

"I just killed a man, and the police are on the way to my office."

"Don't say anything to anyone until I get there. I'm on my way."

How We Are Wired

When my editor read the passage you just did, she had a comment. She wanted to know if my heart rate rose. Did I feel an adrenaline rush? Or break out in a sweat? "Show some reaction" was her suggestion. As I thought about responding to the comment, it opened up a whole can of worms in my mind. I think an emotional reaction would be the norm for most people when they learned of Callie's predicament. But trial lawyers—especially criminal trial attorneys—are not normal people. It's not that we don't feel emotional or empathize with our clients' dire situations on the worst day of their lives. We do, but it's only for a split second. We are trained

> by experience to push past emotions and concentrate on the facts. The who, what, when, where and why of the event. My getting all flustered to an already flustered Callie was not the answer. My job was to control and contain the situation, and I would give her a hug when I got there.

I met Dr. Pagonis two years earlier. She had just left the military and purchased a radiology practice on the South Shore of Long Island. Her two-year plan was to update the equipment in the office and transform it from a run-of-the-mill radiology practice into a state-of-the-art one catering primarily to women. Her goal was to bring the woman's touch to the practice of radiology. With the help of her father, a partner in a New York City brokerage firm, she purchased the newest and best imaging equipment: X-ray, mammography, ultrasound, bone density and magnetic resonance imaging (MRI) from the international leader in radiology equipment, Siemens Medical Solutions.

The second phase of her plan was to transform the nondescript medical office into one that would be welcoming and calming to women. She hired a prominent interior decorator to make her office female friendly. Couches and high-back chairs would replace the traditional waiting room furniture, and original paintings by local female artists would grace the soft pastel walls. A five-foot-tall water feature was to be the focal point of the waiting room.

To accomplish all of this and more, the office was closed for five days. As the office's grand opening was set for Labor Day, September 6, 1993, the preceding Saturday and Sunday would see Callie and her staff putting the final touches on the office. And so it was on Saturday, September 4, when all of her staff, except for the chief radiologist who had called in sick, arrived at 8 a.m. to place the furniture per the designer's floorplan and stock all the medical shelves, as well as the supplies for the clerical and billing staffs.

At approximately 3:15 p.m., Callie received a call from her best friend and referral source, Dr. Judith Locklear, a doctor of chiropractic medicine. Judy was clearly upset as she told Callie that a frail eighty-five-year-old patient, Tim Bonvoy, had come to her office for treatment accompanied by his daughter, Helene. Judy had treated the patient and told him to remain on the exam table until she could get Helene to help her place him back in his wheelchair.

In less than the two minutes it took Judy to bring Helene into the examination room, the gentleman had tried to get off the table himself and fell to the ground. They found him sprawled out on the floor. Judy immediately examined Mr. Bonvoy and noted no lacerations or broken bones. The women got him back into his wheelchair. Judy suggested calling an ambulance to take Mr. Bonvoy to the local hospital emergency room to be checked for spinal fractures,

Cases You Can't Make Up

common when an elderly patient suffers a fall. Helene strenuously objected. She thought an ambulance ride and a long wait in the ER would unduly traumatize her father. The patient agreed with his daughter and said he was "feeling fine."

Judy was not so convinced. She urged getting an MRI, if she could arrange it, from her friend, a radiologist, whose office was located just around the corner.

Reluctantly, Helene agreed to her father's MRI scan "as long as it doesn't take too long." Judy assured her it would not. She then called Callie, who agreed to see the patient.

The trio arrived at her office at about 3:40 in the afternoon. Because her office was not open for patients yet, Callie immediately took Mr. Bonvoy, along with his daughter and Judy into the MRI suite. She explained to Mr. Bonvoy and Helene the purpose of the scan and how the MRI worked. She then helped Mr. Bonvoy out of his wheelchair onto the gurney that slides into the MRI bore. She put two safety straps across the patient's chest to avoid another fall off a table, and he was told not to move once the exam started.

Callie asked Judy to take Helene into her office while she went into the control room to start the exam. The MRI was in ready mode, and the spinning of the magnets could be heard in the exam room, as well as through the intercom in the control room. While Callie had not operated the MRI in a while, she was familiar with its operation because she and the chief radiology tech, the one who was at home sick, had worked together on calibrating the machine this past week.

"Mr. Bonvoy," Callie said in her professional voice, "we are about to start the exam. You will hear the spinning of the magnets increase, and the machine will make two or three loud banging sounds. This is all normal. Just lie back and relax."

Callie started to spin up the machine. A gauge on the control panel showed the MRI magnetic field slowly but steadily increasing from 10 percent on its way to 90 percent of maximum, the strength desired for the spinal exam.

While she was focused on the console gauges, Callie saw something out of the corner of her eye followed by a loud clank. She flipped up the plastic cover over the red button labeled STOP, quenched the magnet and shut down the power. Callie ran into the exam room. Judy and Helene followed. Callie immediately went to examine Mr. Bonvoy. Helene stood silently in shock. Judy took one look at her patient on the MRI table and proceeded to vomit on the newly painted concrete floor of the MRI room.

By the time I arrived, the fire department apparatus and police squad cars had already left. Only two detective cars and a black van marked Medical Examiner's Office remained in the parking lot. I found Callie, who was visibly shaken, sitting on the couch in her office holding a mug of hot tea. Homicide Detective Sergeant Matt Carey sat behind Callie's desk. I had not previously met Detective Carey but knew of him because the county only had six detectives dedicated to homicide cases. After introductions, Detective Carey told me that Callie had declined to make any statement until I arrived but that he, nevertheless, had read her the required Miranda rights.

As soon as the detective left the room, Callie said to me, "I just killed an eighty-five-year-old man." After talking to her for about fifteen minutes, I advised Detective Carey that Callie was too upset to be interviewed at this time. Accordingly, we set an appointment to meet at noon on Tuesday at the homicide bureau.

I drove Callie home and spent the next two hours calming her down and arranging for family members to stay with her. We also agreed to meet on Labor Day to prepare for the interview.

An hour before the scheduled Tuesday meeting, Detective Carey called me and said there were a couple of changes—which he did not sound happy about—that we needed to discuss. First, the meeting would not be held at the homicide bureau but in the district attorney's office. Second, the interview was to be conducted by the deputy chief of the homicide bureau, G. Lawrence Grayston. The tinge in Detective Carey's voice confirmed what I had heard about Assistant District Attorney Grayston.

All lawyers, be they for the defense or prosecution, have reputations in the courthouse community. Some are called straight shooters; others are tough but fair; and still others, out of control. ADA Grayston fell into the third category. He had a reputation for being arrogant, with a holier-than-thou attitude that made even the most tangential witness to a homicide feel they were somehow complicit in the murder. Here, there was no doubt that Callie was complicit.

The issue to be resolved by the district attorney's office was binary: was the death of Timothy Bonvoy an accident or caused by Callie's criminal negligence or the result of her reckless conduct, which could result in the charge of manslaughter in the second degree?

Homicide 101

Without turning the section into a textbook on criminal law, I need to give you a high-level view of the law applicable to Callie's case. She was not being investigated for murder. Murder is defined as "intentionally causing the death of another person." That clearly was not the case here. Rather, the ADA was attempting to determine if Callie acted "recklessly" or with "criminal negligence" in the death of Timothy Bonvoy.

To convict Callie of Manslaughter in the Second Degree, there had to be proof beyond a reasonable doubt that she acted "recklessly." That is, she was "aware of and consciously disregarded a substantial and unjustifiable risk" that death would occur and such disregard constituted a "gross deviation from the standard of conduct that a reasonable person would observe in the situation." For a conviction of Criminally Negligent Homicide, there needed to be proof beyond a reasonable doubt that Callie failed to perceive a substantial and unjustifiable risk that caused Mr. Bonvoy's death and the failure to perceive such a risk constituted "a gross deviation from the standard of care that a reasonable person would observe in the situation."

The difference between these two charges is significant in that Manslaughter Second Degree carries a maximum jail term of fifteen years while Criminally Negligent Homicide carries a maximum of four years in prison.

Of course, all this becomes a legal exercise if it is determined that Mr. Bonvoy's death was the result of an accident, that is, that Callie's actions constituted civil negligence but did not rise to the level of criminal negligence.

The interview in Grayston's office lasted less than an hour. We tried to explain the situation from Callie's point of view, but he was "not interested in hearing any excuses." He reiterated that the patient being treated by Callie managed to get his head crushed by a metal oxygen tank that should never have been in an MRI room and that "by itself, constituted gross negligence."

At the end of the meeting, Grayston announced that he would recommend the DA's office not make the charging decision in this case but would leave it to the decision of a grand jury. In response, I indicated to him that Callie wanted to testify before the grand jury and would file a formal demand to that effect.

More Legal Stuff About the Grand Jury

As I said previously, the purpose of the grand jury is to determine if a crime has been committed and who committed it. However, it's like a one-sided trial. The grand jury only hears witnesses called by the prosecution in support of its case. There is no cross-examination of the prosecution witnesses by the defense and in only rare cases will a witness for the defense be permitted to testify. This is because the grand jury only accuses an individual of a crime and does not determine guilt or innocence. Moreover, to ensure that all witnesses before the grand jury tell the truth, the law gives such witnesses transactional immunity. This means the witness cannot be prosecuted for any acts she testifies to before the grand jury, i.e., the witness is immune from prosecution except for crimes of contempt before the grand jury (refusing to answer questions) and perjury. (This rule is different in federal court, but we will leave that for another day.) That being the case, people who are targets of the grand jury (the possible future defendants), do not get a chance to testify before the grand jury and tell their side of the story.

However, as with all rules, there is an exception. If the target of the grand jury wants to testify, she must waive the right to transaction immunity and will be told anything she says before the grand jury can be used against her at trial. The witness also must know that the prosecutor will be able to ask cross-examination questions after she makes her statement before the grand jury. Also, the grand jury can ask relevant questions of the witness. In a feeble attempt to level the playing field, the law provides that the target may have her attorney present with her in the grand jury room, but counsel may not participate in the proceedings and can only provide advice to the client upon request.

Callie and I discussed the strategy of her testifying before the grand jury at length before she made the final decision to do so. To my way of thinking, the facts were not being contested. It was a matter of what was Callie's state of mind and the only person who could testify to that was Callie.

Preparing a witness to testify in a grand jury consists of many parts.

First, I wanted to make Callie feel comfortable. Most people have never seen the inside of a grand jury chamber, and that name alone—"chamber"—can make people apprehensive. Because a grand jury chamber is located inside the non-public part of the district attorney's office, I could not take her there beforehand. The best I could do was describe the room for Callie in detail. The rear portion of the grand jury room had three rows of chairs in a semicircular, theater-seating configuration. The room was large enough to accommodate a minimum of sixteen to a maximum of twenty-three grand jurors who heard testimony and either voted for an indictment or no true bill (a dismissal). There was a podium located in the right front of the room for the prosecutor, and next to the podium, a table for the grand jury reporter. A single witness chair was the sole piece of furniture in the front center of the room. This was designed to make the witness feel vulnerable and alone facing the grand jurors.

Since Callie had waived her transactional immunity to testify, I would be permitted in the grand jury room with her to advise her if necessary. I would be sitting next to Callie but would intentionally push my chair back about a foot in order to make it look like I was not coaching her testimony.

Our position was simple: this event was a terrible, unfortunate accident and not a result of criminal negligence.

Second, after describing the room, I outlined the sequence of events we wanted Callie to "discuss" with the jury. I intentionally used the word "discuss" because Callie would have the opportunity to tell her story in narrative form before being cross-examined by Grayston. It was important for Callie to speak from the heart and connect with the grand jurors. I made a checklist of topics we wanted to discuss just to make sure she hit them all. Her presentation had to be organized to hit our key points but not come across as a memorized speech.

Third, I wanted Callie to always refer to Mr. Bonvoy's death as "the accident" we believed it was, and not the result of "a gross deviation from the standard of conduct a reasonable person would observe."

Fourth, I made sure she understood, any questions posed by either the ADA or the grand jurors had to be answered truthfully, directly, sincerely and without any equivocation.

Based on Grayston's caustic comments during our interview, I was able to anticipate some of the questions he might ask and had Callie prepared for a response.

Lastly, the grand jurors would also have the opportunity to ask questions we could not anticipate. If that occurred, we would (a) tell the truth, the whole truth and nothing but the truth and (b) fall back on our key position that this event was an unfortunate accident and not a result of criminal negligence.

On the date scheduled, Callie appeared at the grand jury dressed in a dark blue pantsuit with a white blouse. The only jewelry she wore was her wedding ring. Our intent was to make Callie look like the professional physician she was. As the time approached for us to enter the grand jury room, I saw Callie's hand shaking.

I took her hand and whispered, "Remember, every marine is a rifleman." She returned the squeeze and whispered back, "Oorah," the marine battle cry. We walked into the grand jury chamber.

When we entered the chamber, twenty grand jurors were already seated. ADA Grayston opened the case as an "investigation into the death of Timothy Bonvoy" and reminded the jurors that at their previous session they heard testimony concerning this case from police officers and representatives of the medical examiner's office. He then advised the grand jury that Dr. Calliope Pagonis had requested to testify before the grand jury and had signed the waiver of immunity. With that, he introduced us to the grand jury. Grayson then asked Callie to stand, raise her right hand and swear "to tell the truth, the whole truth and nothing but the truth, so help you God." With the legal formalities out-of-the-way, Grayson asked if she wish to make a statement to the grand jury. Callie responded, "Yes"

One of the unwritten rules of grand jury practice from the defense perspective states: the first thing a client should do is go through a lengthy and slow description of his or her background to introduce themselves to the grand jury. The point is to plant the idea that such an outstanding individual could not, in any way, have committed the criminal act alleged. In Callie's case, that rule would dictate we start off with a college degree (from Yale), and then go to a medical degree (from Duke), then medical training (at Johns Hopkins), followed by awards received and finally a full recitation of her military career (from captain to colonel).

I decided not to follow the rule. I wanted the jury to know right away that Callie was a knowledgeable physician who cared for her patients. We would get the jurors' attention by showing Callie's true personality—something you cannot manufacture because jurors see right through that sort of lie. This is how Callie started her presentation:

"My name is Callie Pagonis. I am a radiologist. I am here before you today because I am responsible for the death of my patient, an eighty-five-year-old man named Timothy Bonvoy. I am responsible for the accident that took Mr. Bonvoy's life. I am responsible for the lapse of my supervision that led to his gruesome death. Was I civilly negligent? Clearly, the answer is yes, or Mr. Bonvoy would not have died. However, I am here to tell you that I was not criminally negligent."

You could hear the proverbial pin drop as Callie said those words. She did not sound rehearsed. She spoke from the heart. We had decided not to run away from the fact that Mr. Bonvoy died a horrible death from blunt force trauma to his skull. We could not avoid admitting this brutal fact because the medical examiner's testimony had already established it, but we could describe the horrible scene Callie saw when she ran into the MRI suite.

"I was in the MRI control room when I thought I saw a flash out of the corner of my eye and then heard a loud clank. I looked up and saw an oxygen tank suspended in the middle of the MRI's magnetic field. I immediately hit the emergency button to commence the shutdown of the MRI. When I got to Mr. Bonvoy's side, I saw half of his skull and face were sheared off by the force of being hit by a two-foot steel oxygen tank when it flew into the MRI core. I was horrified and in shock and recall Dr. Judy Locklear standing next to me, vomiting on the floor. It was horrible. There was no way I or any other physician was going to be able to save Mr. Bonvoy's life."

I believed that if we told the stark truth here, at the beginning, her sincerity would carry over to the rest of her testimony.

How were we going to explain the accident? I decided to use the work of social scientists who analyze disasters ranging from aircraft crashes to building collapses to explain what occurred in the MRI suite. Briefly, social scientists believe that there are multiple small failures that lead to a major accident. Individually, none of them is sufficient to cause a disaster. Only when a chain of seemingly unrelated failures occur, does a catastrophe result. Callie mentioned some of the unrelated failures that led to Mr. Bonvoy's death:

✦ The rush to complete the office in two days for its grand opening.

- ✦ The illness of the radiology tech who would have been in charge of outfitting the MRI suite on that Saturday.
- ✦ The floor plan laid out by the interior decorator (who was not a medical person) noted the placement of "an oxygen tank next to the crash cart."
- ✦ The clerical person who took the ill radiology tech's place scrupulously followed the interior designer's floor plan and did not appreciate the fact that only special non-ferrous oxygen tanks are permitted in an MRI suite.

Callie spent nearly thirty-five minutes telling her story, slowly and completely, to the grand jury. As she was testifying, her voice and demeanor conveyed the pain she was feeling in such a way that it appeared that every juror was feeling her pain. I felt she had done the best she could, and I was thrilled that her direct testimony went so well. Surprisingly, when she completed her statement ADA Grayston said he had no questions. Even more surprisingly, none of the grand jurors raised their hand to ask a question. By the time we left the chamber, Callie's blouse was sweat stained, and she was shaking as my paralegal Wendy walked her to my car for the trip to our office.

While Callie was recuperating in our office, my secretary buzzed me. "I know you're not taking calls, but you will want to take this one. It's Grayston."

The ADA was direct. "Gregg, the jury voted a no true bill. The case is over, and I want you and the doctor to know that Detective Carey and I agree with the jury's decision."

Now that the criminal charges had been resolved, Callie authorized me to contact her medical malpractice insurance carrier and demand that the civil case brought by the Bonvoy family be resolved quickly and fairly.

The last hurdle we had to jump was at the New York State Board of Professional Medical Conduct. It had filed a complaint against Callie for practicing medicine with gross negligence on one occasion. Because Callie did not want to fight the allegation by going to a hearing, we entered into a plea agreement with the health department. The department fined her the maximum penalty of $10,000 and suspended her license until she completed a course of education in MRI safety.

No matter what penalty was imposed, Callie told me the greatest penalty is that she will have to live with the fact that her neglect led to a death.

A penalty only suffered by a physician who truly cares about her patients.

Sometimes It Happens

Those old enough to remember the 1957 TV show *Perry Mason* will fondly recall Perry's cross examinations of prosecution witnesses were always executed so brilliantly that a witness's testimony helped the defendant win the case. All trial attorneys yearn for that "one moment in time," but it rarely occurs. However, it sort of happened to me.

My client, Frank Burns, was charged with driving while intoxicated (DWI). In New York at that time, you could be convicted of driving while intoxicated if you operated a motor vehicle on a public street with a blood alcohol level of .10 (today's level is. 08) or in an intoxicated condition. After he was arrested, Frank refused to take a breathalyzer test that calculates a person's blood alcohol level from a breath sample.

In Frank's case, since there was no breathalyzer result, he was deemed to be intoxicated by the observations of the arresting officer and was charged with DWI. He was offered a plea to the charge and would receive an agreed-upon sentence of a period of three years' probation and a $500 fine. Burns refused the plea deal because he was adamant that he was not driving intoxicated.

So, the trial began.

The prosecution's first and only witness at trial was the arresting officer, Samuel Flagg. His testimony would constitute the entirety of the prosecution's case and was designed to show that Burns was driving a vehicle while in an intoxicated condition beyond a reasonable doubt.

As soon as Flagg was called to the witness stand, it was obvious that he was angry about being in court, and his body language seemed to scream, "How dare you doubt my arrest?"

Once he sat down, he had a smirk on his face. His deep-set eyes, bald head and bushy mustache made him look like a pissed-off gargoyle. His condescending attitude was so plainly visible to the point that I believe he made the jury feel uncomfortable. I loved it.

This case boiled down to whether you believed the officer or not, and it's hard to believe someone you don't like.

In sum, Flagg recited the usual litany officers are trained to testify to in DWI cases: He saw the defendant driving a 1970 Ford Falcon on Hempstead Turnpike, a four-lane highway, at 1:30 a.m.; the driver was in the right-hand lane but was swerving into the left. The officer pulled the driver over. He smelled the odor of alcohol on his breath. The driver's speech was slurred and his eyes were glassy. When asked, the driver told the officer that he had "two vodka shots on the rocks during his dinner at the Davenport Press." Flagg said he ordered the driver out of the car and administered the standard field sobriety tests, which "the defendant failed miserably." Accordingly, he made the arrest.

As the prosecution's entire case relied upon Burns's failure to pass the field sobriety tests, the ADA had Flagg testify about what the tests were, how he administered them and how the defendant performed. The standardized field sobriety tests, as used then, consisted of a battery of three tests: finger to nose, the one-legged stand, the walk and turn. These tests are called "divided attention tests" and, according to their developers, are easily performed by sober drivers. The test developers also claimed that an officer trained in the administration of the test could correctly identify an alcohol-impaired driver 90 percent of the time.

Specifically, the tests require a driver to listen and follow instructions while performing simple physical movements on the theory an intoxicated person will have difficulty with the tasks requiring their attention to be divided.

Officer Flagg grudgingly testified as to what he directed Mr. Burns to do. "I told him to stand feet together with his arms at his sides, then to extend the pointer finger on his right hand, bring his right arm up and touch the tip of his nose with his pointer finger.

"Next, I told him to take nine steps heel to toe along a straight line, then turn on one foot and return in the same manner to the start. I was looking to see if he could keep his balance while listening to instructions or if he took the wrong number of steps. Then I told the defendant to stand with arms at his side and lift one foot about six inches off the ground and to count 1001, 1002, 1003 until I told him to put his foot back down. I was looking for any swaying, using his arms to balance, hopping to maintain balance or putting the foot on the ground.

"Based upon Mr. Burns performance of the three tests," Officer Flagg concluded in a much louder voice, "he failed all three tests."

I planned to argue in summation that even sober people could fail the tests Flagg administered, especially people like my client. He was fifty-seven years old, short, had a fat stomach and worked as a CPA sitting at his desk most of his workday. He never exercised other than puttering around the house.

Dr. John McIntyre, an orthopedic surgeon, was prepared to testify he had treated Frank for his knee condition for the past three years. There were times during this treatment that Frank had difficulty walking and experienced a pain level of "eight out of ten" in his right knee. Eventually the pain got so bad due to bone-on-bone contact in his knee, Frank had no choice but to have surgery. McIntyre was further going to testify that Frank's left knee was likewise arthritic and would also need a replacement soon.

We had also lined up Joe Peligro from the well-known catering establishment Thoma's in Great Neck. Mr. Peligro had been a bartender for ten years and was now the vice president for wine and spirits at Thomas. We intended to call him to testify that based on his experience, an individual who had two shots of vodka on the rocks would not have any alcohol smell on his breath. Mr. Peligro was going to inform the jury, "Alcohol itself has no smell or odor. It is the hops and barley that give beer its smell. The aging of grapes in oak barrels adds aroma to wine. Other aging methods for spirits like Scotch or bourbon that age in charred oak casks or the botanicals added to gin are what give off their distinctive aroma." It was going to be Mr. Peligro's opinion (assuming I could get him qualified as an expert) that it was highly unlikely a person who had two shots of vodka—or for that matter even four shots of vodka—would have any smell of alcohol on their breath.

My final argument to the jury was going to be: "Jurors you heard about the field sobriety tests and how they were administered. Try them in the jury room and see if you pass."

But I never got the chance to say those words.

I was not impressed with Officer Flagg as a witness or his testimony, so I thought I would take a chance. Believing Confucius was correct when he said a picture is worth a thousand words, I decided to cross-examine Officer Flagg in an unorthodox method.

"Your Honor, may I have the court's permission to have Officer Flagg leave the witness box and stand before the jury?"

The room in the district court building where we were trying this case was no more than forty feet long and eighteen feet wide. The space between counsel's tables and the jury left about five feet between the furniture and the jury box. That's where I wanted the witness to stand.

The court granted my request, and Officer Flagg stood in front of the jury while I questioned him. My plan was to take Flagg through the three tests he administered to my client to show the jury how difficult the tests were.

Q: Officer Flagg, you previously described the three standardized field sobriety tests you administered to my client, Frank Burns, correct?
A: Correct.
Q: Officer, would you please show the jury exactly how you directed Mr. Burns to perform the finger to nose test?
A: Yes.

I told the defendant to stand with his feet together; arms by his side; extend his pointer finger on his right hand; bring the right arm up and touch the tip of the pointer finger to the tip of his nose.

As the officer raised his right arm to touch his pointer finger to his nose, the jurors let out an audible gasp.

Officer Flagg missed his nose. His pointer finger found the area between his nose and his bushy lip.

My next question was an obvious one: "Officer Flagg, are you intoxicated?"

The ADA stood and shouted, "I object, Your Honor."

The judge overruled the objection and then with a grin on his face looked over at Officer Flagg and asked, "Officer, are you now intoxicated?"

Flagg responded, "No, Judge."

As I was sitting down, I said, "I have no further questions, Judge."

The jurors looked like they had seen a bomb explode. The ADA asked for and got a recess.

Upon returning to the courtroom, without Officer Flagg, he dismissed the case.

Thanks, Perry.

Cases You Can't Make Up

To Pee or Not to Pee, That Is the Question

I was driving back to my office on the Long Island Expressway from New York City at noon and, of course, traffic was crawling as I left the Midtown Tunnel. The car phone rang. It was a friend of mine who practiced corporate law in New York City. He had a problem.

"My client will call you as soon as I hang up. The hospital he works for wants to suspend him on the spot. This is your expertise. Please help him."

As I approached the merge with the Brooklyn-Queens Expressway, the call came in. Through a thick British accent, I heard: "Naclerio, I am Dr. Birdwhistle. I am a surgeon.

"The hospital wants me to pee [i.e., give a urine specimen] for a drug test on the spot or they will summarily suspend my admitting privileges. What shall I do, sir?"

This clearly was not going to be a simple yes-or-no answer. I was able to pull off to the shoulder of the road to take the rest of the call.

Me: Dr. Birdwhistle, are you at a location where no one else can hear our discussion?
Client: Yes.
Me: Just to be sure, Doctor, are you retaining me to represent you so everything we say in this conversation is protected by attorney-client privilege?
Client: (*clearly coached by my corporate friend*) Absolutely. You are my barrister. Can we please get

to the point? I only have five minutes to decide whether to pee or be suspended by the hospital.

Me: Doctor, in the last forty-eight hours have you taken any medication or substance that would impair your ability as a surgeon?

Client: Are you mad, sir? I was scheduled to perform surgery this a.m. I do not even drink coffee, tea or any other caffeinated beverages twenty-four hours prior to operating. And I certainly do not use alcohol or illegal drugs. *(annoyed)* I told you that I am a surgeon and I need your answer now!

Me: OK, if you believe your urine test will be negative for any inappropriate substances, then and only then provide a urine specimen for the hospital. If you are completely convinced that the urine test will be negative, also demand a blood test.

Client: Hold on ... *(a brief mumbled exchange)* I'm told the tech will be here to administer the urine test and draw a blood sample within the next thirty minutes.

Me: Fine. Now that we have some time, please tell me what caused the hospital to believe you are under the influence of some intoxicant.

Client: It's a rather long story, Naclerio, but I will give you the abridged version. As I said, I am a surgeon here at University Hospital. Not just a surgeon, mind you, but I am a full professor of bariatric surgery. Do you understand what that is?

Me: I am not exactly sure what that specialty entails. Can you please enlighten me?

Client: Bariatric surgery is a procedure that assists in weight loss by making changes in the digestive system. It is prescribed for patients who are severely overweight to lower their risk of life-threatening problems such as heart disease, stroke and fatty liver disease. There are many types of bariatric surgery, and I am the world's leading authority in the duodenal switch technique.

Me: Understood. So why is administration in effect accusing you of operating under the influence of an intoxicant?

Client: My surgery is very technical and requires an experienced mind, steady hands and state of the art instrumentation. As the world leader in this delicate surgical procedure, I require the best surgical instruments available to achieve the results I demand. University Hospital is reaping hundreds of thousands of dollars from grants I bring in and hundreds of thousands more from the patients who come to this hospital for my expertise. My practice brings significant income to the hospital, yet they refuse time and time again to purchase the equipment I require to operate properly. I have gone to my section chief, department chair, the administrator and even to the chairman of the board of trustees to get what I need. Despite promises upon promises to do so, no equipment has been forthcoming.

    Sir Winston Churchill said, "If you have an important point to make, don't try to be subtle or clever. Use a pile driver. Hit the point once, then come back and hit it again. Then hit it a third time—a tremendous whack." That's what I did this morning.

Me: So exactly what did you do this morning?

Client: Today, I had a case scheduled for 8:30 a.m. that had to be canceled, but the OR staff was unaware of it. I arrived at the operating theater today at 8 a.m. to ascertain if the requested and promised surgical instrumentation was being sterilized. Upon inquiry, I was advised that the promised equipment was not there ... was not there. (A pause to let me absorb the impact.) In response, at 8:15 a.m. I entered the scrub room and donned my head and foot coverings. Thereafter, I spent approximately fifteen minutes scrubbing my hands. However, I intentionally did not put on the traditional operating room gown and entered the operating theater straight away in my scrub suit.

As I entered the OR, the anesthesiologist and the scrub nurse were present and sternly warned me to get my surgical gown so as to not break the sterility of the room. As they approached me, they stopped quickly in their tracks when they noticed I was only wearing my scrub tops and no trousers.

Me: Doctor, did you say you entered the operating room without trousers?

Client: That is absolutely correct, sir. I was nude from the waist down, and her majesty's jewels, which I might add are quite impressive, were on full view. The lady anesthesiologist said she was appalled but nevertheless had a good look-see. With all the commotion going on, the charge nurse called a timeout, which requires a pause in all activity, and immediately notified administration.

A junior administrator came running into the operating theater without following sterile procedures and in effect contaminated the entire operating suite. He started yelling at me, and I was ordered to put on my trousers and report to the chief of surgery's office. It was at this meeting with my chief that I was told I had to provide a urine specimen or else I would be summarily suspended.

That's when I called you.

Dr. Birdwhistle did in fact provide a urine and blood specimen for the hospital. Both samples proved negative for a slew of tests the hospital ordered. The hospital, of course, did their best to keep the incident quiet for fear of losing patients. It took two weeks, but Dr. Birdwhistle finally got his surgical equipment.

Apparently, Sir Winston was correct.

CHAPTER FOUR

Divine Justice

Her name was Parker Divine, and she most certainly was.

Born in Yorkshire, England of parents working for the United States State Department, Parker was educated in London and graduated from Oxford University. When her parents were transferred back to New York, she joined them and attended Columbia University School of Law, where she graduated number nine in her class. Parker could've easily gotten a job with a Manhattan white-shoe law firm in New York; however, she decided to grace the halls of the Midsommer County Courthouse with her legal ability and charm.

Parker stood six feet tall, had a ramrod straight model's posture and her peaches-and-cream complexion was accentuated by her signature blonde ponytail. When she spoke, her language was not a New Yorker's English. It was British.

To us, she was English royalty. Many of the single lawyers in the courthouse desperately sought Parker's attention, but unfortunately for them, she stayed unattached.

After working for two months at the DA's district court trial bureau, Parker attracted the attention of Michael Landis.

Landis was chief of the DA's County Court Trial Bureau. His office was located in the executive suite on the top floor of the courthouse, proof that he was the third-most powerful person in the district attorney's office.

Landis did not like his colleagues, and he showed a constant disdain for them any time he could. The feeling was mutual since most of his co-workers despised his condescending attitude and knew that he occupied such a lofty position solely due to the personal request of the county's political leader. It was also clear to the senior leadership of the office that Landis intended to use his position as a stepping stone to higher political office. Specifically, Landis was being groomed for the state governor's office when the current occupant's term expired in three years.

Landis fancied himself a ladies' man and was currently going through a hard-fought divorce due to his wife's discovery of his affair with a secretary (some seventeen years his junior) who worked in the county clerk's office.

And then he met Parker. He asked her to assist him on one of the biggest cases being prosecuted by the office. It was clearly not her legal expertise that Landis sought or needed, given the fact she was only six months out of law school, but he was looking for another conquest, this time in the DA's office itself. The office had an anti-fraternization policy, but

Landis knew he was above the rules established by the DA.

Parker accepted the offer to move from her basement office to the top floor. Soon, a working relationship turned into a secret dating relationship. That is, if you were to believe the courthouse gossip mill, which had a 97.5-percent reliability rating.

Over several months, the Landis-Parker team progressed from meetings in the office's war room, to closed-door meetings in Landis's office, then to Saturday afternoon working meetings that morphed into Saturday dinner dates, ultimately culminating in Parker making them breakfast the next morning at Landis's condo.

Landis's conduct infuriated the DA, but he was powerless to stop it. Fortunately, the matter was solved when Michael Landis was appointed to the New York State Supreme Court (a trial court hearing felony indictments) to fill out the term of a judge who suddenly—at the party's urging—decided to retire early. The judicial appointment was for ten years, but Judge Landis could not care less. He knew he had three years to brand himself for the race to the governor's mansion in Albany.

Even before Judge Landis took the bench, he decided that he would create his image as the county's hanging judge. He believed that such a reputation would serve him well not only to secure his party's nomination but also would be a tangible plank in his law-and-order platform for the election run. To achieve this image, Landis felt he had to make changes to his persona. He chose to grow an Abe Lincoln-style beard, cut his hair in the form of a crew cut, and adopted walking with a hand-carved five-foot walking stick from his ancestral home of Scotland. Lastly, he knew he had to get rid of the blonde he was secretly dating, Parker Divine.

Like most people Landis met and used to benefit his ego or career, Parker Divine became expendable. It mattered not that Parker was falling in love with him. All that mattered was she would be a liability in the governor's race. His opponent would attack his ethics in dating a subordinate employee in the DA's office, some twenty-five years his junior, in clear violation of the DA's published anti-fraternization policy.

Moreover, and more important to Landis, was that Parker's beauty would only accent his correctly perceived ugliness in the countless photos that would be taken during the campaign. Like a quart of milk that was going sour, Parker had to be kicked to the curb. While he was still working on the scheme to do so, he fantasized he could use the services of Vinny Boombats, who was currently serving a life sentence in Sing Sing State Prison.

Earlier in his career as a prosecutor, when Landis was still in love with the law rather than himself, he convicted Vinny of four counts of murder in the first degree. Vinny, the owner of a legitimate business, Long Beach Cesspool Contracting Company (whose catchy slogan was, "Your Number Two Made Us Number One"), had a second job as the button man for the Testafresca crime family. When the family determined someone to be a liability, Vinny would see to it that the liability ceased to exist by disappearing at the bottom of one of his newly constructed cesspools.

Landis needed his Parker liability to disappear, but it had to be done legally.

Nevertheless, he thought, a guy is allowed to dream.

From the beginning of his term, Landis wanted all the attorneys who would appear before him to know what to expect. He asked to meet with representatives of the district attorney's office, Legal Aid, the assigned counsel program as well as the presidents of both the county bar association and the criminal court's bar association. The reason for this meeting was not disclosed, but the general feeling was that it was thought to be a "get to know you" meeting.

Wrong!

In a brief ten minutes, with no questions or discussions allowed, Justice Michael Landis laid down the rules of his court, the Landis Rules.

The rules were as simple as they were draconian:

1. All pleas offered by the DA to an indicted defendant must contain a felony or else the judge will not accept the plea.
2. All pleas to a felony will result in a jail sentence:
   A *first-felony offender* would be sentenced to up to one year in the county jail.
   A *second-felony offender* would receive a minimum of four years in state prison.

A *third-felony offender* would receive a minimum of seven years.
3. No sentences of probation would be imposed, no matter what the circumstances..
4. If a defendant chose to go to trial and was convicted, that defendant would receive the maximum sentence permitted by law.

"There are no exceptions to these rules!" Landis roared to end the meeting.

It was clear that Judge Landis chose to ignore two axioms that permeate the criminal justice system: "Justice tempered with mercy" and "Sometimes good people do bad things." Under the Landis Rules, if you were arrested and had the misfortune of having your case assigned to his courtroom, young or old, male or female, first time or repeat offender, the die was cast. You were going directly to jail.

Since an indicted individual's case was assigned to a judge on a random basis, a defendant stood a one-in-thirteen chance of having his case assigned to Landis. While similar cases given to any one of the other twelve justices gave a defendant a meaningful chance for a plea bargain with the possibility of a short sentence in the county jail or even probation, such an opportunity did not exist in Justice Landis's courtroom.

The Need for Plea Bargains

Plea bargaining is prevalent for practical reasons and benefits all parties concerned. Defendants can avoid the time and cost of defending themselves in a trial, the risk of harsher punishment if convicted and the negative publicity a trial could generate. The prosecution saves time and expense of lengthy trials, which frees up staff to work on other cases, and the court gets to handle more cases and reduce the always-present backlog. Moreover, both sides are spared the uncertainty of a jury trial. In most counties and the federal system, 90 to 95 percent of indicted cases are disposed of by plea bargains.

 Remember, the grand jury that indicted the case against Tom Defendant only heard evidence produced by the district attorney's office. In the grand jury, the prosecution witnesses are not cross-examined, the validity of any search and seizures are not adjudicated by a neutral magistrate and no witnesses are presented by the defendant.

 As so eloquently stated by a former chief judge of the New York State Court of Appeals, Sol Wachtler, the district attorney has so much influence over a grand jury that "by and large, they could get a grand jury to indict a ham sandwich." (It is interesting to note that Judge Wachtler himself was indicted for making threats to a former girlfriend and her daughter and received fifteen months in federal prison.)

Thus, during a plea bargain conference with the judge and the prosecutor, the defendant gets the opportunity to point out the weaknesses of the people's case, offer evidence the defendant would produce at trial and bring forth certain extenuating factors including his or her prior record and community involvement as well as any assistance rendered to law enforcement.

Based upon these and other factors, the district attorney may decide to reduce the original felony charge to a lower-level felony or even a misdemeanor. Also, on rare occasions, the facts brought forth by the defendant at the conference may warrant the prosecution to reevaluate their case and could lead to the case being dismissed.

Once the reduced plea is offered, the judge can then take into consideration the defendant's background, injury to the victim or community caused by the defendant's actions and many other factors in deciding the appropriate sentence to be imposed.

The criminal justice system and the public also benefit by needing only a handful of judges to dispose of the large number of criminal cases that reach the court's docket.

Scenes From a Criminal Lawyer's Notebook

Under Justice Landis's Rules (now being called the "Injustice Landis Rules" around the courthouse), his calendar of pending criminal cases increased significantly. Defendants who were told that if they accepted a plea, they would be doing four years in state prison, did the math and many decided to roll the dice, hoping that in any hearings, critical evidence would be suppressed, or their trial would result in an acquittal or hung jury. If you were offered a sentence of four years on a plea or the max of seven years if you lost the trial, would you roll the dice?

So, for the next four months the Landis Rules created pandemonium in the courthouse while felony cases piled up on his docket. Despite pleas by the DA himself, the senior supreme court justice and the chief judge of the office of court administration to abandon the rules, Landis stood firm. When he was named in a lawsuit filed by the county's Legal Aid Society on equal protection grounds, he saw it as a badge of honor. Landis was enjoying the publicity, and his plan to gain the reputation as the county's hanging judge was right on target. Indeed, Landis was looking forward to the upcoming Criminal Courts Judges Conference since there was a session on the program focused on his new approach to criminal justice. This three-day conference would serve as his debut for his election bid for governor.

The first four months of Landis's judgeship were also difficult for Parker. She found herself being marginalized by the DA's office. She didn't have the trial experience to be in county court, and without Landis, she was relegated to do anything but trial work. She even toyed with asking the DA to let her go back to district court but then realized it would only confirm the courthouse gossip that she got her job by sleeping with Landis. No one had any proof of the affair but gossip does not need proof to be a fact. The pressure Parker felt only increased when she saw less and less of Landis since he was now too busy to see her except for the few times he stopped by Parker's apartment for an overnight stay. Parker still labored under the delusion that she was Landis's girlfriend. When she asked about going to the conference with him, Landis told her, "It would not look good." She abided by his decision but ever so slowly started to come to the realization that although she was in love with Landis, he had other plans, and she was not part of them.

Parker sulked all alone the weekend of the judges conference and spent a lot of time fighting the reality that her relationship with Landis was coming to an end. It would come to an end sooner than she thought. Before she arrived at work Monday morning, the gossip mill was overheating. Her friends were avoiding her, and she felt the cold chill when she spoke to some of the office staff. She remained unenlightened until one of her former colleagues in district court called her to say Landis had been seen at the conference "hanging all over his new secretary."

"Yes," the friend continued, "that eighteen-year-old with the Dolly Parton figure."

That was the last straw for Parker, and it pushed her over the edge. She raced across the football-field-sized parking lot between county court and supreme court and made a beeline for Justice Landis's courtroom on the third floor. Then, composing herself, she calmly and professionally walked up to the clerk in charge of the courtroom and flashed her district attorney's badge saying she was told to go directly to the judge's chambers. Once she passed the elderly clerk, she opened the door to Landis's chambers and came face-to-face with "Dolly," who was seated behind her computer. Words ensued—mostly from Parker—and voices escalated.

Parker told Dolly to stay away from "my boyfriend." The expected "he's not your boyfriend, bitch" followed. As Parker started to go around the desk to confront Dolly, Landis heard the commotion and interposed himself between the two combatants. The three voices continued to escalate until court officers rushed in. Before they could restore order, Parker changed her target to Landis. She tried to smack him in the face while he used his walking stick to fend off her attack and—most likely unintentionally—pushed Parker backwards. She fell to the floor. Court officers escorted Parker out of the room while Landis hugged and consoled his terrified new girlfriend.

In the fifteen minutes it took Parker to walk back to the district attorney's office, Landis had called the DA and demanded Parker Divine be fired. It was the one time the DA and Landis fully agreed, and as soon as Parker entered the office, a district attorney squad detective manning the reception desk told her, "The boss wants to see you. Now!"

The meeting was very brief. The DA fired Parker for conduct unbecoming an assistant district attorney and told her all her personal effects would be boxed up and sent to her home. Then, the final humiliation: "Detective Harper, please escort Miss Divine out of our office."

Shaken and totally embarrassed, Parker was marched out of the DA's office under the gaze of her friends and coworkers. She spent the next several months at her parents' brownstone in Brooklyn Heights battling depression and the realization that her legal career was over.

Then fate intervened in the form of the most respected criminal attorney on Long Island, Serlano Spardo. "Sale," as he was called, was both a superior trial attorney and truly a renaissance man. To say that Sale marched to his own drummer would be an understatement. He could be easily spotted in the courthouse wearing his signature black bowler hat—which he would tell you, "is a symbol in Britain that represents ordinary things that possess secret powers and challenges us to rethink the surrounding world as we know it"— a dark blue suit and hand-tied bow tie.

Any discussion with Sale revealed a thoughtful insight and remarkable perspective, whether he was discussing the Yankees, a Puccini opera, the current New York City Ballet season or the skills exhibited by Linda Lovelace in her new movie, *Deep Throat*. He was also a five-star chef and enjoyed having friends come to his Lower East Side fifth-floor walk-up apartment for a gourmet dinner ending with his signature chocolate mousse for dessert.

He grew up on an estate not far from Sagamore Hill, Teddy Roosevelt's summer White House, not because his family was wealthy but because his father was the gardener for the estate and his mother its manager.

Sale went to college at Princeton University, obtained a degree in psychology and then joined the Peace Corps for two years. Upon his return, he graduated from the University of Chicago Law School, one of the top law schools in the country. He went back to New York City and went to live on the Lower East Side not far from Washington Square Park in Greenwich Village. He did so because the rent was cheap. Twenty-five years later, Sale does not pay any rent. He owns the building. And the two next door.

Sale currently had three cases pending before Justice Landis. At least two of the three cases would have received a sentence of probation or at most six months before any other judge, but Landis would not hear of anything short of a four-year prison sentence. On this day, March 17, St. Patrick's Day, all three cases were on the trial calendar. The appearance was expected to be merely ministerial with the court setting trial dates.

When his cases were called, Sale asked to approach the bench. Landis, who was annoyed that Sale's client would not take a plea, sarcastically asked: "Sale, are you prepared for trial?"

Sale: No, Your Honor, I am not prepared to proceed.

Landis: That is not acceptable. You know you are on my trial calendar, and these three cases are some of the oldest ones in my courtroom. They must and will be tried as your clients refuse to plead guilty. The trials will start two weeks from today, March 31, and you will try these cases seriatim. If you don't know what that means, it's back-to-back-to-back. Am I clear, Mr. Spardo?

Sale: Exquisitely clear, Your Honor. The cases will be tried, and tried as you directed, back-to-back-to-back. Unfortunately, Judge, at my age of seventy-four such a trial schedule would be too taxing on my health, so I have retained trial counsel for all three cases.

Landis: (*getting angrier*) You will not, I repeat, will not, delay the start of these cases commencing March 31 by getting new counsel. Is that clear?

Sale: Judge, I don't intend to delay the trial. I am here to say we are ready for trial on all three cases and to introduce to the court my trial counsel ... Ms. Parker Divine.

Parker removed her sunglasses, stood up from the crowded spectator's area and walked to counsel's table. The court personnel could see Justice Landis's blood pressure go through the roof.

Landis: You two, approach the bench.

Parker, Sale and the assigned assistant district attorney did so quickly, so as to not further annoy the explosive jurist. From the bench, the judge scowled at the lawyers and told the court reporter, "Off the record." It was thanks to Sale's photographic memory we know what occurred next.

Landis: What type of sick joke is this, Sale? You and Miss Divine better be ready to proceed on March 31 or I will hold each of you in contempt of court.

Sale: Your Honor, Miss Divine has been in my employ for one month now, and her sole responsibility is to prepare for trial on the three pending cases. She has spoken to each client personally, reviewed our file, spoken to our witnesses and is thoroughly prepared to proceed.

Landis: *(fuming)* Are you telling me that your clients, who hired the best criminal trial attorney in the county if not the entire state, have agreed to let this attorney who has never tried a criminal case, let alone a serious felony, try their case?

Sale: Yes, Your Honor. *(handing the consents to the clerk)* I have their consents for the substitution of counsel right here and will be pleased to present a copy to the court.

Landis: I don't know what you're up to Sale, but these cases will start in two weeks' time, or you and Miss Divine will sit in a county jail cell till they start. Anything further?

Sale: Just one more matter, Judge. Miss Divine...

Divine: Good morning, Your Honor. We only have one motion we would like to make before the trial begins. It's a rather simple motion and can be disposed of this morning if the court so chooses. It is a motion to recuse you as the trial judge based on the grounds that you and I worked together as colleagues in the district attorney's office. As you well know, a judge should disqualify himself from any case to which he has a personal connection that might create the risk or appearance of impropriety.

Landis: (*completely ignoring Parker and directing his comments to Sale*) Bullshit! You know as well as I do that working as colleagues in the district attorney's office is not grounds for recusal. I will let you make the motion today, and I will deny your motion for the record ... Today!

Sale: If Your Honor intends to deny our oral motion, we will withdraw it and submit papers and a brief in a formal written motion—

Landis: (*cutting Sale off*) And you will get the same decision.

Sale: Very well, Your Honor, but I want to advise you that our formal motion will contain several other grounds for recusal besides what we were prepared to put on the record today.

If we are forced to submit a formal motion to the court, which will become part of the public record, our motion will contain additional grounds, some of which I would like to outline briefly for Your Honor.

First, you are twenty-five years Miss Divine's senior and were the third most powerful man in the district attorney's office. You took an obvious novice, someone who was only a lawyer for four months, to work on the largest drug case in history of the DA's office as your assistant.

Second, not only did you have a working relationship with Miss Divine, you also cultivated a social relationship with her. That social relationship then proceeded to a dating relationship, which was in contravention of the district attorneys anti-Fraternization policy.

Third, that dating relationship then proceeded to a sexual relationship with Miss Divine while you were still married to your wife, which constitutes a crime of adultery as set forth in section 255.17 of the New York State Penal Law.

Finally, during a verbal altercation between Miss Divine and your current girlfriend-slash-secretary, you intervened and pushed Miss Divine with your walking stick, causing her to fall backwards to the floor.

While this court may not think this pattern of sexual harassment and inappropriate sexual conduct rises to the level for recusal, I'm sure the appellate court, to which we will immediately appeal, will feel differently. Moreover, all of this and perhaps more will become part of the public record and be of interest to *The New York Times* and, my personal favorite, *The New York Post*.

With each item Sale ticked off, Landis saw his bridge to the governor's office being destroyed. He stopped the conference at the bench and had the parties go back on the record.

Landis: After further consideration, it is the opinion of this court that due to the fact that Miss Divine and I worked as colleagues in the district attorney's office the motion to recuse myself from this case is granted.
  Next case.

Although the words uttered by Parker Divine were not included on the record, at least four people reported her last word to Justice Michael Landis: "Checkmate."

News of Sale's victory spread throughout the criminal court bar like a bolt of lightning. Other criminal defense attorneys who represented clients with assets, immediately retained Parker as their trial counsel and made motions to recuse. As Justice Landis himself had established the precedent that he would recuse himself on any case in which Parker Divine was trial counsel, five more motions were granted in one week alone, with more no doubt to follow.

The Legal Aid Society represented the largest number of cases on Justice Landis's calendar. Clearly, these clients did not have the means to retain Parker Divine, but she was so inundated with work from other private attorneys, she couldn't have taken the Legal Aid cases if she wanted to, and she really did want to.

Roscoe Ellman, the chief attorney at Legal Aid, knew that merely working as a colleague in the DA's office was not generally a good reason for recusal. There had to be more to it, and Ellman decided to subpoena Parker Divine in the civil lawsuit against Landis that was currently pending. Parker decided that by cooperating in the civil lawsuit, she would be able to assist all the indigent clients who had their cases assigned to the hanging judge.

When Landis found out, he saw the writing on the wall. He knew if Parker was deposed on the record, all of what Sale said and more would become public record, and the headline in the local newspapers would read, "The Pervert Hanging Judge." Landis knew that he would be lucky if he remained on the supreme court bench if that story broke.

To avoid Parker's deposition, Landis asked the senior supreme court judge to speak to Ellman and immediately resolve the lawsuit. An agreement was arrived at whereby the lawsuit was withdrawn and Landis would be reassigned to the supreme court part that only heard civil cases. All of Landis's criminal cases would be reassigned to another supreme court justice. The new justice, upon taking over Landis' calendar, immediately rescinded the Landis Rules and operated her courtroom in the same manner as the rest of the criminal court judges in the county.

At dinner one evening, Sale and Parker discussed the principles behind their success.

As he sipped his Louis Roederer Cristal champagne, Sale opined it was Sir Isaac Newton who won their case. "Parker, it was Newton's third law of motion—for every action there is an equal and opposite reaction—that helped us win the case."

"I have to disagree, Sale. I believe it was William Congreve who helped us win the case."

"Are you referring to his play *The Mourning Bride?*" Sale asked.

"Yes," she replied and quoted, "Heaven has no rage like love to hate returned nor Hell a fury like a woman scorned."

CHAPTER FIVE

Did I Tell You About …?

During my forty-year-plus career practicing criminal law, several strange events occurred. I want to tell you about four of them. The first is based upon hospital gossip told to me by several people who claimed it actually occurred. The next three, I know to have occurred. They happened to me.

The Case of the Chapel Cover-Up

Sister Mary Suzanne, a Catholic Sister of Mercy, spent her entire vocation as a teacher of children in the seventh and eighth grades. This night found her in room 314 of St. Paul's Hospital. Now eighty-three years old, she was suffering from the results of a stroke that caused right-side paralysis and compromised her vocal abilities. As she had for the last sixty years, she placed her trust in the Lord and sought the solace of prayer. Sister used her left hand to grab the TV remote on her bedside table and scrolled to the Chapel Channel. The time on the wall clock read 2:17 a.m. when the chapel feed appeared on her screen.

Being a religious institution, the channel was a twenty-four-hour live feed from the chapel attached to the hospital. When services were not being broadcast, it showed the altar and a large cross that invited prayer and meditation. Sister Mary Suzanne, fingering her rosary beads, was in prayer for some ten minutes or so when she let out a loud scream.

The sound caught the attention of the night charge nurse, who ran into the room. She saw a shocked expression on the nun's face as Sister pointed to the TV screen. The nurse froze as she looked at the screen.

A man in a white doctor's coat and a woman dressed in nursing whites stood behind the altar and engaged in passionate kissing that was at least rated PG-13. Then it got worse. The man started to unbutton the nurse's dress button-by-button and slowly eased it off her shoulders. It fell to the floor. The display was now R-rated. Finally, lifting the lady onto the altar, he commenced a rhythmic thrusting, which pushed the show to X-rated.

By the time the nurse returned to her desk and called hospital security to report the incident and the officer on duty rushed to the chapel, the tryst was over and the chapel again returned to its intended purpose.

As per the hospital's procedures, Nurse Lorraine Buckman immediately contacted the administrator-on-call, Kyle Kendell, who was also the hospital's chief administrator. Wiping the sleep from his eyes, he told Nurse Buckman to meet him in his office in two hours. Kendell needed the extra time to contact the chairman of the hospital's board of trustees "concerning the desecration of the chapel by hospital employees." The chairman's direction was brief and to the point: "Resolve this indiscretion immediately and without any adverse publicity befalling the hospital and the church."

The administrator, with the assistance of Nurse Buckman, soon found out that Nurse Tabitha Chambers was one of the stars of the late-night TV show. Kendell directed that both Chambers and Buckman meet with him in his office at the start of their night shift. Once confronted, Nurse Chambers, a single 23-year-old, admitted her role in the scandalous conduct but also sought to blame Dr. Kerry Byrne. In her defense, she told Kendell that the doctor had been asking her for sexual favors for several months. She also reported the word among the young nursing staff was, if they wanted to succeed at the hospital, they had better cave into Byrne's demands since he was the senior partner in Town Interventional Cardiology Group, a practice that brought all its cardiology and cardiac surgery patients to the hospital and as such was a power to be reckoned with. While Kendell was furious at Byrne, he first had to handle the Chambers situation. He excused Nurse Buckman from the meeting and sat down with Tabitha Chambers. He proposed a quick solution to the problem:

She could be fired for cause because she left her nursing station without prior permission, and she engaged in a sexual act in the hospital chapel. A firing for cause would require the hospital to set forth all the reasons for the termination. To avoid embarrassment to herself and her parents, with whom she resided and who were very active in the church, Kendell suggested it would be in her enlightened self-interest to resign instead. No reason had to be given.

As Tabitha was not solely at fault, Kendell proposed that if she signed a nondisclosure agreement with the hospital in which she would agree not to disclose any of the facts concerning her employment or commence a lawsuit against the hospital, he would be able to help her get a position at University Hospital's pediatrics department. Additionally, her new position would be on the dayshift and at a salary one level above her current paygrade. To work this minor miracle, Kendell had to call in several favors he had done for his counterpart at University Hospital. But it had to be done.

Tabitha thought about the offer for fifteen minutes and agreed to sign the documents requested by the hospital.

The next meeting Kendell had was with Lorraine Buckman. A similar deal was made with the charge nurse, who traded her silence by virtue of a nondisclosure agreement for a transfer to the day shift and an administrative role in the nursing department. She was older and wiser than Tabitha and signed on the dotted line immediately.

The third phase of the cover up was completed unwittingly by Dr. Andrew Letap, the physician caring for Sister Mary Suzanne. That morning, during his rounds, Nurse Buckman told him that the sister was having bad dreams and hallucinations while on the anti-anxiety medication he had prescribed and suggested he change the current medication. Without any discussion of these adverse reactions with Sister Mary Suzanne, he just changed her medication and countersigned the last entry made in her medical chart, which read, "Patient reports having a bad dream last night." It was signed "Lorraine Buckman, RN."

With three of the four witnesses to the indiscretion silenced, Joshua Brodie, the chairman of the board, decided to speak to Dr. Byrne himself. Brodie had recently served as special assistant to the president for legislative affairs in the Reagan administration and was responsible for shepherding the administration's legislative agenda through Congress. He had learned horse trading from the best—politicians. During their meeting, when the topic of sexual harassment came up, Dr. Byrne made his threat.

"If the hospital plans to take any action against me for these baseless allegations, I will direct my practice, which as you know consists of ten cardiologists, to immediately cease using St. Paul's Hospital for our patients. We will do all our cardiology and cardiac surgery cases at University Hospital. As you well know my practice's admissions generate significant dollars for your hospital. I can shut that off in a minute, and you cannot weather it financially."

Brodie did not flinch. He sat back in his chair and calmly described the facts as he saw them. "If you take the action you just threatened, the hospital will have no choice but to summarily revoke your admitting privileges and file a complaint with the New York State

Medical Board. If that occurred, the entire community would be made aware of the fact a forty-three-year-old married man with three kids under the age of fifteen not only sexually harassed young nurses on the surgery floor but forced one naive twenty-three-year-old nurse into a sexual liaison. Moreover, you had the unmitigated gall to conduct your extramarital affair not only in the chapel, but upon the consecrated altar no less. By your sinful acts you desecrated the church that many of our fellow townspeople attend. The adverse publicity generated by your actions would not only affect your wife and children but would also cause the God-fearing people of our community to seek care from the other cardiology groups in town. Such a loss of patient volume would most likely cause your partners to force you out of the very lucrative cardiology business you founded to save their livelihood."

With the threat of mutual destruction, the parties agreed to conduct business as usual with the hospital taking a very strong but very unofficial position that such conduct by Dr. Byrne would not be tolerated in the future.

The entire cover-up took less than seventy-two hours to complete. Nevertheless, to this day, hospital gossip still tells the story of the Midnight Desecration and the cover-up by the good-old-boy network.

It's up to you whether to believe the story or not.

I believe it happened.

Oh, I forgot to mention that my seventh-grade elementary school teacher, someone I stayed in touch with over the years, was Sister Mary Suzanne.

Learning the Lingo

I started working at the Legal Aid Society two weeks after taking the July 1971 bar exam. Since the exam results would not be known until mid-January 1972, my job was that of an intern doing legal research and determining if individuals referred to Legal Aid for representation were determined to be indigent. This determination was made after the prospective client filled out a financial questionnaire. Legal Aid staff usually filled out the forms by conducting an interview with the accused or their family.

The process began in arraignment court where the judge would advise the recently arrested person of the crime charged against them, their right to counsel, that counsel would be provided if they could not afford a lawyer and the decision of what type of bail would be set.

Most days, there were ten to fifteen individuals who needed to be interviewed. This task was managed by senior Legal Aid Investigator Paul Reese. Paul was a retired New York City police detective who always had a scowl on his face and was always in a cranky mood.

Paul could complete the eight-page financial form in less than four minutes by telling the prospective client to just answer all questions yes or no. However, the two interns assigned to him thought the form was a sacred document requiring a lengthy response to each question. This drove Paul crazy when the number of prospective clients filled his office and then spilled out into the hallway. Things were especially hectic the day after Labor Day, and Paul was yelling at me to get the financials done "now." I just handed him my fifth form of the morning when Paul snarled, "Naclerio, take this case ... Dickie Wavier," and handed me the complaint that charged the crime.

I didn't have time to read the charge but only to find my client so as not to incur the "Wrath of Reese." I went into the hallway looking for my client calling his name, "Mr. Wavier, Mr. Wavier, Dickie Wavier."

Getting no response, I put my head into Reese's office and called out the client's name again but this time softer, "Mr. Dickie Wavier." Still no response, but I saw Reese stand up ... and come straight at me. His usual scowl was gone, and he was fighting back a laugh.

"Dummy, his name is not Dickie Waiver. He is a dickie waver. He's charged with indecent exposure. He waved his dickie at some lady at the Roosevelt Mall. Don't they teach you kids anything in law school?"

The Human Lie Detector

Today, the US Army's AH-64 helicopter, better known as the Apache, is the world's best attack helicopter. It is highly maneuverable, heavily armed and the backbone of the army's ground-support capability. But not so much when it was born in 1983. According to a report issued by the Army Inspector General's Office, the Apache had over a hundred design deficiencies that made it horrible to fly.

One of these deficiencies pertained to the four twenty-two-foot main rotor blades made from steel and a composite material glued together to maximize strength and minimize weight. The case started with a civil lawsuit charging fraud brought by the United States against Hermes AeroSpace. The small fifty-person company, solely owned by Dustin Fox, took its name from the Greek god of speed and was primarily involved in fabricating steel to be used in airplanes. As the civil suit progressed, the government uncovered facts that led it to open a criminal investigation into both the Hermes firm and Fox individually. That's where I came into the story. I was retained to be Fox's defense attorney.

The investigation was headed by Major Steve Morgan, a helicopter pilot prior to being sent to law school by the government. The major was cross-deputized as an assistant United States attorney and made a request to interview Fox before any decision was made whether to proceed with the criminal case against him. This was going to be a difficult case because (a) Morgan personally knew two of the Apache test pilots who were seriously injured in crashes; and (b) there was no doubt that Hermes overcharged the government. Hermes had certified that the steel it sold was purchased from a foundry that fabricated steel using what was known as the "vacuum degassed method" when, in truth and in fact, the steel was produced using the cheaper "electric arc method."

The case was going to come down to a matter of intent. That is, could the government prove that Hermes, and specifically Mr. Fox, had the criminal intent to defraud the government and prove it beyond a reasonable doubt?

Major Morgan already knew we had retained the services of Professor Peggy Champagne of Rensselaer Polytechnic Institute to be our expert witness. After Professor Champagne and her staff analyzed the steel sold by Hermes, they concluded that while the steel did not meet the military specification (Mil Spec) in the manner it was fabricated, it did meet or exceed every other Mil Spec for durability and strength. The case hinged on Fox's state of mind, i.e., did he intentionally supply less costly steel to the army and passed it off as the more expensive Mil Spec material? Or did he believe the steel met all the Mil Specs except the method of manufacture and was similar if not better than the material ordered?

Major Morgan wanted to meet Fox and cross-examine his story. If we didn't go for the interview, the odds were Fox would be indicted. If we did go for the interview, perhaps we would have a chance to convince the major to proceed civilly against the company and not criminally against Fox. This was our goal because a felony conviction could not only lead to a jail cell but would also bar Dustin Fox from bidding on all government contracts and, in effect, destroy his business.

After much discussion and weighing of the pros and cons, we decided that the interview with Major Morgan would be the more prudent course to follow. However, before it took place, I would prepare Fox for the interview. This was going to be our one shot to avoid indictment, and we had to be very deliberate in our planning. Our guiding principle was to tell the truth, the whole truth and nothing but the truth. If Major Morgan believed we were lying about any part of the transaction, he could conclude we were lying about everything.

More importantly, and most likely, along with the major, an FBI agent would be present at the interview. Lying to an FBI agent constitutes the separate crime of obstruction of justice, which in itself is a felony.

Being prepared for this kind of interview requires more than just an accurate representation of the facts. As Mama says, "It's not what you say, but how you say it." Our preparation had to not only include a detailed recitation of the facts as we saw them; we also had to anticipate the questions Major Morgan would ask on cross-examination.

I carefully explained to Dustin the rules of engagement for this meeting.

First, he would have to listen to the question asked, understand the question or ask for clarification and answer just the question without any extraneous statements.

Second, for us to convince the government that Fox was telling the truth, I would have to let Major Morgan have a shot at him without me butting in or have it appear I was coaching the witness. In short, Dustin Fox was going to fly solo on this mission.

Lastly and most importantly, was the prime directive, "If you get stuck answering a question, always tell the truth."

I'm sure you're going to want to know whether we practiced for the interview. The answer, of course, is yes. We practiced his statement several times until I was confident that Dustin projected the honest person he was. Then came the hard part: he had to be able to answer the questions I anticipated the major would ask.

I now became the prosecutor and hammered Dustin. I took his statement and cross-examined him on what he said. I started from the end and went backward. Most people who tell lies have their story memorized going from beginning to end. By starting at the end and going to the beginning, it is possible to catch someone lying. I also had a colleague of mine, who was a former federal prosecutor and who Dustin did not know, subject him to a stiff cross-examination. This was Dustin's one shot to avoid indictment, and we had to be prepared—and we were.

Besides going over the facts of this case, I asked Dustin if there was anything in his background that I should know about prior to the meeting. I asked him if he had ever been convicted of a crime. His response was definitive: no.

I also told him that the FBI had probably done a background check on him, and I needed to know if he had any skeletons hiding in his closet such as a history of alcohol or drug abuse, domestic violence or even stealing money out of the basket at church. His response was again, no.

The day before we were scheduled to leave JFK Airport for Phoenix, Dustin called: "I don't think this is important, but you should know about it.

"When I was a senior in high school, I worked as a stock boy and cashier after school and on the weekends for Modell's Sporting Goods. During the winter break, Modell's always ran a special sale on skis. You could get a pair of boots, bindings and specific lower quality skis for $120. I was trying to be a big shot in my high school, so I told several of my friends, to come to Modell's and take advantage of the sale. And did they ever take advantage of the sale. They would go to the rear of the store and pick up a pair of the top-of-the-line boots and skis, which had the retail value of $370, and bring them to my cash register. I would then only charge them the sale price, and they would walk out with a higher grade of merchandise.

The sixth time I did this, I was caught by the manager and confessed. The police were called and, since I did not have the money to reimburse Modell's for the property stolen, I was charged with larceny in juvenile court. The case was resolved with a sentence of probation, and I was told the case was sealed and could never be used against me. This happened over thirty years ago. I don't think its relevant, but I wanted you to know."

―≪≪◆≫≫―

The next day at 8:30 a.m., we sat in the Phoenix office of Major Morgan. He immediately apologized saying our meeting had to be adjourned till noon. The FBI agent, a polygrapher, who was to attend our meeting, was coming in from Dulles Airport in DC, and her flight was delayed due to a snowstorm. This was the first time that Morgan had indicated that he wanted a polygraph examination of Dustin, and I told him I did not like this unprofessional surprise. He did not respond. My gut told me this was out of character for him to spring a polygraph examination on us right before the meeting and after we had traveled halfway across the country to get there. Something just didn't seem right to me. Why was the polygrapher coming from DC? Any trained polygrapher could have stepped in to conduct the examination. Something was up, but I could not put my finger on it.

At noon, the meeting was again adjourned to 2 p.m. because the polygrapher was having trouble making connections to Phoenix. At 4 p.m., Morgan advised that the polygrapher was not going to be able to make our meeting, but he had decided to proceed without her.

For the next hour the meeting went according to plan. Dustin stated our position clearly and referred to several exhibits we made available to the government supporting our position. At the conclusion of Dustin's statement, the major requested we take a break before he started his cross-examination. As we left the conference room, Morgan asked to speak to me privately. He took me to his office and said he only had one question to ask Dustin and asked for my cooperation.

When the meeting started again, Major Morgan sat directly across from Dustin. He told Dustin he had just one question to ask him, and to ensure that I was not coaching him in any way, he asked whether Dustin would have any objection if I stood behind him while he asked his question. I nodded my consent and Dustin agreed. I stood up and positioned myself about a foot behind Dustin's chair.

Morgan then proceeded to ask his one question: "Have you ever been arrested anytime in your life?"

I knew the answer to the question (and now, so do you). I hoped that Dustin would remember the prime directive.

Dustin took a long pause before he answered, "When I was a senior in high school, I worked as a stock boy and cashier after school and on the weekends for Modell's Sporting Goods. During the winter break, Modell's always ran a special sale on skis ..."

After Dustin's answer, the interview concluded, and Major Morgan said he had to discuss the case with the superiors and would advise us of their decision within two to three weeks.

True to his word, I received a call from the major who told me that the government had declined prosecution of Dustin Fox personally; however, they would proceed civilly against his company, Hermes AeroSpace.

We talked some more, and I asked him what the story was concerning the polygrapher. While Morgan was not willing to discuss whether the polygrapher was really supposed to attend a meeting, he told me he thought the "human lie detector" was much more reliable than any machine. And that he strongly believed in the legal axiom:

Falsus in Uno, Falsus in Omnibus.

Latin for "False in one thing, false in everything."

The major told me that if Fox told the truth about a minor and irrelevant issue that happened over thirty years ago that no one was supposed to know about, the odds were significant that he was telling the truth when it came to the steel his company sold to Boeing.

Thank God, Dustin remembered the prime directive.

It's something we all would do well to follow.

⤙⤚ Observe by Watching ⤙⤚

"You can observe a lot by watching."
–Yogi Berra

It was the summer of 2002, and I was driving to work when the newscaster on a local radio station reported that one of the largest companies on Long Island, Stewarts Staffing, was being investigated by the US Department of Justice for violating the federal Anti-Kickback Statute. The government was alleging Stewarts used its wholly owned subsidiary Lucie Physical Therapy (Lucie PT) to orchestrate a kickback deal with Challenger Health, a national for-profit hospital chain. The essence of the deal was that Lucie PT would sell all its freestanding physical therapy offices located in the greater Atlanta area to Challenger Health at a price substantially below fair market value. In return, Challenger would cease providing outpatient physical therapy for its patients living in southern Florida and refer them all to Lucie.

From a strictly business point of view, the transaction was a stroke of genius orchestrated primarily between the presidents of Lucie PT and Challenger Hospital. However, if the Lucie PT offices were intentionally sold at below fair market value in return for obtaining Challenger's patients living in southern Florida, the transaction was clearly a violation of the Anti-Kickback Statute, and those involved could face a fine of up to $100,000 or imprisonment of not more than ten years or both. To compound the situation, the Federal False Claims Act, at that time, could civilly punish the same conduct with fines up to three times the amount of loss sustained by the government plus a penalty of a minimum of $5,500 and a maximum of $10,000 per claim filed.

A few hours after listening to the news, I received a telephone call from a lawyer in Florida with whom I had given a presentation at a recent National Healthcare Anti-Fraud Association meeting. Gabe Scuderi told me that he was representing Stewarts in the investigation.

"Sounds like a real tough case," I said.

Gabe replied, "It only gets worse. The government wants to make an example of this case and is looking to indict the officers of Lucie PT or Challenger

Hospital to establish a precedent that they will use to hold individuals as well as corporations liable for kickback violations in the future. That's where I need your help.

"Stewarts has offered to pay the legal fees for the Lucie PT president, Robert J. Ostinato, because he could be facing up to ten years in a federal penitentiary if convicted, but he will be selecting his own attorney. Five attorneys have been recommended to him for his consideration. The first three were found not acceptable. You're number four."

I had represented several New York companies for kickback violations, but this would be a case with national exposure. I was ready to tackle a case of this size, and I was confident that my team could handle it. All I had to do was convince Mr. Ostinato.

I had to prepare quickly to meet with him the next day at 4 p.m. Gabe emailed me the key documents from the government outlining their case as well as correspondence with the attorneys representing Challenger Health. The more I learned about my prospective client, including information provided by Gabe's staff, the more I realized his surname was really a clue to who this person was. "Ostinato" is translated from the Italian as "someone who has an unreasonable attachment to a belief; stubborn."

This was going to be fun.

I arrived at Mr. Ostinato's office fifteen minutes before the appointed time only to be told by his administrative assistant that an emergency requiring Mr. Ostinato's attention had just occurred. I was about to ask if we should reschedule the meeting when Ostinato came charging out of his office shouting to his assistant, "Get the CEO and the CFO in my office immediately."

Because I was standing right in front of him, he looked at me and said, "Counselor, we are running a little late. Please come into my office study. It's more comfortable than this waiting room."

The room I was directed to looked more like a den in a residence. It contained two leather chairs and a small coffee table. The walls were lined with eight-foot-high bookcases holding books and memorabilia. It was here I sat alone while Mr. Ostinato slowly gathered his minions for the critical meeting in the adjoining conference room. I tried but could not hear most of the discussions. I could hear Ostinato, though, when he bellowed out orders. As the meeting dragged on, I perused the books and items on the seemingly never-ending bookshelves.

The meeting lasted thirty minutes. In that amount of time, I learned a few things about the president: he rarely took the advice of others, liked intimidating people and enjoyed calling his adversaries "dickheads." Finally, he walked to the room where I waited. He sat down and said, "Let's get this meeting out of the way. Talk to me."

I proceeded to say three or four sentences about my firm and then started the usual spiel about my credentials to handle this high-profile case when I was unceremoniously interrupted.

"I know about your firm, and I am impressed with your credentials. You will learn I do my homework. But the key question I wanted answered is why I should retain you to represent me. You don't know anything about me other than what you probably read on my press bio or heard from the company's lawyers."

Up until thirty minutes earlier, he was absolutely correct. I chose to avoid the question (a mistake on my part) and proceeded to respond that if the allegations against him were true, he not only would be fired but would face civil suits with penalties in the millions of dollars and probably do time in a federal prison. It would be my strategy that we work together on his defense and that after we discussed the issues, I would make all the calls on strategy while he had the last say on testifying and resolving the case. I reiterated we would need to work together and become a team for the sake of his career and his family. Again, I was interrupted.

"What do you know about my family?" he growled. I felt I was losing the battle with Ostinato and decided to fight fire with fire.

I looked him straight in the eye and told him, "You're married and have three children. Two boys and a girl. Your family likes to ski, and Squaw Valley in Idaho is one of your favorites. In the summer you enjoy spending time on your power boat. Your daughter loves horseback riding and is a competitive rider. Your two sons are fencers, one in épée and the other in saber."

As I spoke, he had a look of amazement on his face. He was anxious to hear more and sat back in his chair, crossing his right leg over his left knee.

"You like to play golf, but your putting needs a lot of work. And lastly, your locker at the golf club is number 229."

I sat back in my chair and waited for his response.

"None of that is public information. Not even my executive staff knows some of those facts. Where was that information printed?"

I hastened to tell Mr. Ostinato that I didn't have to read anything. "All that information is right here before us. While you were engrossed in your meeting, I just walked around the study and observed. There are pictures of you, a woman and three kids skiing in a frame stamped Squaw Valley. There is a similar picture of the five of you on a power boat. You have photos of your daughter jumping a horse. And as for the photo of your two sons who fence holding their weapons, I fenced in college and know the difference between an épée and saber. There are also photos of you and others playing golf, and there's a putter against the wall in the corner, which means you practice putting when you can. Besides, everyone believes they are horrible at putting. And lastly, when you cross your legs, the bottom of your shoe, between the heel and sole, had the number 229 written in black marker. That's your locker number at the golf club so the clubhouse attendant knows which locker to return the shoes he just polished."

For once, Robert J. Ostinato had nothing to say.

The next day I got a call from Ostinato himself.

"I would like to retain you to represent me. I need someone who can think out of the box, handles pressure and pays attention to details. Since we're going to see a lot of each other over the next several months, please call me Bob."

Bob's words were indeed prophetic as we spent the next two years battling the US Attorney's Office in the Middle District of Georgia and the Southern District of Florida. To complicate matters, the Florida US attorney himself decided to get involved in the investigation and seemed to be more concerned with garnering publicity by bringing the largest anti-kickback case in the country than predicating his case upon a solid foundation of evidence. We spent months producing documents, witnesses (including Bob) and expert testimony—all showing that the transaction between Lucie PT and Challenger Health was a legitimate business transaction and not a kickback. Lastly, the US attorney asked us and counsel for Lucie PT to produce a white paper outlining our legal position before December 1. The case had dragged on so long, I did not expect a decision as to whether Bob would be prosecuted before the end of January. On December 23, I was getting ready to leave for our office's Christmas luncheon when a call came in.

I immediately recognized the voice as that of the assistant US attorney, who was the lead on the case in Florida. I remember thinking this guy was a real dickhead for calling me right before Christmas to tell me my client was indicted. We spoke quite a few words, but I can only recall, "I called to wish you and Mr. Ostinato a very merry Christmas and I also have a present for Mr. Ostinato. Tell him we're closing his investigation."

As Tiny Tim would say, "God bless us Every One."

CHAPTER SIX

Revenge Is a Dish Best Served Cold

You've heard it said, revenge is a dish best served cold. Let's look at a case that proves it.

It was the first week of December 1993. I took the elevator to the sixth floor, turned left, walked to the glass wall and turned right. Forty-seven paces down the hall. The door was on the right. I had not been in this building for five and a half years, but I knew my way blindfolded.

The sign on the door was the same—State of New York, Medicaid Fraud Control Unit—except for the name on the next line was Sandra Palazzi, Regional Director.

The last time I saw that sign, the name on the door was mine.

I no longer had a key card to the unmarked door that led into the director's private office, so I had to enter the small waiting room and wait for the receptionist who took her sweet time to open the three-by-four sliding glass window. She asked for my name. I wanted to say, "I ran this place for twelve years, and I'm here to play Let's Make a Deal with Sandy Palazzi and Peter Spore," but decided instead to just give the information she requested.

The reason for my trip down memory lane was Dr. Luis Raphael, a psychiatrist who was arrested in an undercover sting operation and charged with the felony of grand larceny in the second degree and related misdemeanors for allegedly stealing $15,000 from Medicaid by billing for services he did not render. The overbilling was attributed to visits that never occurred or billing for an hour of psychotherapy when, in fact, thirty minutes or less of care was rendered.

The case against him was strong. There were tapes of office visits by undercover officers posing as patients; billing forms and progress notes signed by the doctor; and the fact that only two people worked in his practice—him and his wife Olga.

Raphael was facing a maximum of seven years in prison or one year in the county jail, although the more reasonable sentence of probation or three to six months in jail was probable. More of an issue was the fact that the state would revoke his medical license if he pled guilty to a felony.

In my first meeting with Dr. Raphael, his small stature and meek demeanor made me think of Mister Peepers as played by Wally Cox in the 1950s sitcom. In his Spanish-accented but perfect English, he calmly and readily admitted the overbilling. His one goal was to dispose of his case quickly. I was to make sure the case did not go to a trial, no matter what the cost. When I began to give him my analysis of the case, he unexpectedly shot up from his chair and wrung his hands, saying repeatedly, "It was my wife! My wife!" He then composed himself, sat down and let me go on with my presentation.

As he was about to leave, he again started wringing his hands and repeated his mantra: "It was my wife! It was my wife!" I did not understand his behavior, especially when in a matter of a second or two, he again regained his composure and thanked me for my help. It occurred to me, his wife was the real culprit. That would explain his insistence on no trial.

Two weeks later, I had the unpleasant experience of meeting the wife. Mrs. Olga Raphael towered over her five-foot-three husband, was twice as wide and could be, at best, described as domineering. There was no doubt that she ran both the practice and her husband. Although we only spent twenty minutes together discussing the practice's medical and billing records, it was long enough for me to understand she hated the prosecutor's office, the Medicaid program in general and the doctor's psychiatric patients in specific. I am sure I made her hate list, judging by her attitude.

In accordance with my client's wishes, I began to negotiate a plea deal. The attorney general wanted my client to plea to a felony plus restitution of $15,000 and an agreement to take no position on sentencing.

I did not think Palazzi would dismiss the case against my client, but you never know the answer to a question until you ask. Thus, I asked that the criminal case be dismissed and that we proceed civilly with an offer to pay restitution in the full amount charged of $15,000 plus the usual civil penalty of three times the amount of gain or $45,000, for a total sum of $60,0000.

As expected, the AG rejected my offer of a civil resolution of this case, saying, "You need to plea to a felony."

What if, I countered, we were able to provide information on another physician who was stealing many times the amount charged against Dr. Raphael?

I went on to present information (without specifying names or locations) concerning a friend of Dr. Raphael who was also a psychiatrist. About five months earlier, the friend had approached Raphael and asked him for a $500,000 investment to become a partner in a sober house the friend operated. The purpose of a sober house is to provide a living arrangement for alcohol and drug addicts who are going through rehabilitation. The idea is to keep the addicts out of the environment that caused them to become addicted in the first place, and the concept has proven to be successful. In this case, the resident's monthly rent was guaranteed as it came out of the Supplemental Security Income received from New York State and was signed over to their landlord.

When Raphael told his friend he did not wish to make a real estate investment, his friend told him there was more to the deal than just providing shelter.

The second part of the deal would be that the residents would be required to attend three therapy sessions a week at Dr. Raphael's office where they would attend group therapy sessions, but he would be able to bill Medicaid for individual one-hour sessions.

The friend had been doing this for the past year at two of his sober homes and was making significant money because if the sober house residents did not avail themselves of his therapy they would be immediately evicted from the premises. In order to make even more significant money, the friend was looking for investors to buy three more sober homes, and that's why he reached out to Dr. Raphael.

Fortunately, Raphael declined to participate in the scam. Unfortunately, he failed to record the conversation with the friend.

Palazzi was very interested but—as is usually the case with plea bargaining— made a counteroffer. She would dismiss the case if Raphael would wear a wire and engage in incriminating conversations with his colleague.

The next day when I relayed the prosecutor's offer to Raphael, he became very agitated and said he could not wear a wire without having a nervous breakdown.

I looked for a compromise.

Dr. Raphael would make a call to see if the investment was still available, and if it was, he would introduce an undercover Medicaid fraud investigator to his friend. If their undercover operative was able to secure sufficient evidence to indict the other psychiatrist, the AG would offer Dr. Raphael a plea to a misdemeanor and join in our request for a sentence of probation in addition to the payment of full restitution plus interest.

Dr. Raphael performed the required tasks, and the deal was done. All that was left was to meet with the judge assigned to the case, tell him of our plea negotiations and get his agreement to sentence Dr. Raphael to probation.

The matter was assigned to Judge Clancy Malloy who agreed to accept the misdemeanor plea and committed to sentence Dr. Raphael to three years' probation, based upon the AG's recommendation. Three weeks later, full restitution of $60,000 paid, Dr. Raphael pleaded guilty to a misdemeanor, and a date was set for sentencing.

Six weeks later the case of *State of New York v. Luis Raphael, MD*, was on Judge Malloy's calendar for sentencing. So far everything was running as planned, and I did not expect anything to go wrong.

I should have known better.

Judge Clancy Malloy was a bit of a contradiction. He started his legal career as a public defender and then spent ten years as an assistant Suffolk County district attorney where he headed the major offense bureau. Then it was off to private practice where he and his partner only practiced criminal defense. Although his eighteen-year criminal practice was financially successful, Clancy wanted to end his career as a judge. When he first took the bench, the book on the judge said that he would be more favorable to the defense than the prosecution due to his most recent occupation and that his tendency was to be more liberal in his philosophy and demeanor. Although the book was usually correct, it wasn't this time.

Clancy Malloy kept his courtroom on a tight schedule. His calendar of cases was called promptly at 9:30. If you, the attorney, were not there to answer the 9:30 calendar, your case was adjourned to second call, which could be anytime between 11:30 and 12:30. This put a dent in your day as you now had to wait around in the courthouse and could not handle any other matters you had waiting for you in your office. If counsel still wasn't present when the case was called the second time, Judge Malloy would issue a bench warrant for the arrest of the lawyer's client even if the client was present in the courtroom. The poor soul who had paid his lawyer a fee to represent him was taken into custody by uniformed court officers and put in a holding cell located behind the courtroom until his lawyer appeared. The tardy attorney would be told his case would be called at two o'clock while his client sat in a cell and was offered the standard baloney sandwich for lunch. Needless to say, most if not all the lawyers coming before Judge Clancy Malloy were never late.

The judge, whose first name means "warrior" in Gaelic, cut a striking appearance as he sat on the bench. His square jaw, snow-white crew cut standing a half inch straight up over his ruddy face and his ramrod posture made quite an impression of strength. The same was true of the way he handled attorneys who wanted to conference their cases with the prosecutor. In most courtrooms, lawyers who had requested a conference with the judge would take seats in the empty jury box and wait to be called into chambers one by one. Judge Malloy changed that way of doing business. In his chambers, eight seats were placed in a semicircle around the judge's desk for defense counsel. The ninth seat, closest to the judge, was for the assistant district attorney. Malloy would enter the room and hang his black robe on a hook next to the door. Now the judge was seen in his true attire: a long-sleeve flannel shirt and dungarees. Deep down, he was a fisherman like his father, grandfather and great-grandfather. Often Malloy would sneak out during his lunch recess to go fishing in the river half a mile from the courthouse. Moreover, a seven-foot harpoon hung on the wall behind his desk. It had been used by his great-grandfather when he sailed on whaling ships out of Sag Harbor in the 1850s. It was still in use by the judge, meaning he would figuratively use it to jab the lawyers who appeared before him, especially those who were unprepared. Assistant Attorney General Peter Spore and I were spared his barbs because we had both tried cases before Malloy in the past and I had also met him several times at bar association functions. I really got to like his crusty attitude ... or so I thought.

―⋘♦⋙―

On the Friday before Memorial Day, Raphael and I were present in Malloy's courtroom at 9:15 for sentencing. Because it was the start of a holiday weekend, the calendar was light, and we were second on the list. The judge took the bench promptly at 9:30, and the clerk began to call the calendar.

Clerk: People versus Luis Raphael for sentencing.
Me: Good morning, Your Honor. We are ready for sentencing.
Judge: Mr. Naclerio, I am placing this case on the second call calendar. Next case.

Surprised, I looked at Spore who could only shrug his shoulders.

At 11:30 we were present in court as the clerk called my case.

As I stood up and before I was able to take one step to approach the bench, the judge spoke to the clerk: "Mark this case for 2 p.m."

Something was clearly up, and after he left the bench, I asked the clerk if I could see the judge in chambers. His response was quick: "Gregg, Judge Malloy does not want to see you."

Dr. Raphael was beside himself. If we had a deal, why were we being stalled by the judge? After all, he did nothing wrong. "It was my wife, my wife."

At two o'clock, the courtroom was empty except for Dr. Raphael, Peter Spore and me. The case was called, and Judge Malloy asked both Spore and me to step up to the bench.

The judge said, "Gentlemen, I am not sure that I will give the defendant the promised sentence of probation. Therefore, I will let him withdraw his guilty plea and proceed to trial on the felony indictment or he can proceed to sentencing with no promises by me."

I was shocked and needed to consult with my client. I told Dr. Raphael that we should seek an adjournment of the sentence so we could further consider our options and try to find out what the judge was up to. He adamantly refused.

He was not going to trial under any circumstances and did not want to lose the opportunity to plead to the misdemeanor. I asked him to reconsider his position, but there was no changing his mind. He was going through with the sentencing, and it was going to be now.

At the bench, when I advised Judge Malloy of our decision to go forward with the sentence, he looked directly at me and said, "Naclerio, you better be really good and put everything you want me to consider on the record like you always do. Probation is not a foregone conclusion for your client. *Capisce?*"

I assured him I understood.

Something clearly was up, but I could take a hint, and I did just what the judge suggested. I placed on the record all the reasons that would justify a sentence of probation. I explained the fact that Dr. Raphael had made full and complete restitution to Medicaid, paying three times the amount of his theft in penalties and interest to the state. Moreover, he cooperated with the attorney general's office, which led to the arrest of an individual charged with Medicaid fraud worth three-quarters of a million dollars. Lastly, I informed the judge that the attorney general's office was joining in my application for probation. Assistant AG Spore confirmed my representations to the court and joined my application. Then, it was Judge Malloy's turn to speak.

"Mr. Raphael. You are a thief, and I don't think you deserve the title of doctor. So let me address you as Mr. Raphael. I have been weighing all day whether you deserve a sentence of probation or should go to trial on the felony charge of grand larceny. After much soul searching, I have reached a decision. Mr. Raphael, based upon your guilty plea to the misdemeanor of petty larceny, I hereby sentence you to a probationary period of three years with a special condition ... (a long pause) six months in jail."

Before the words "six months in jail" finished echoing through the empty courtroom, two court officers grabbed Dr. Raphael by the shoulders, placed handcuffs on his wrists and hustled him out. As I approached the bench to speak to the judge, all I could hear was the doctor reciting his mantra: "It was my wife, my wife."

When the judge stepped off the bench, I politely but forcefully told him that he had made a mistake in pronouncing the sentence. "The law only permits a special condition of sixty days in jail for a misdemeanor. A six-month jail sentence is a special condition for a five-year probationary sentence in the case of a felony. The sentence you just pronounced is illegal. You made a mistake."

"I made no mistake," Malloy shot back, raising his voice. "I intended to send him to jail for six months and give him a sentence of three years' probation. If you think my sentence is illegal, you can always appeal my decision. For now, he goes to jail. Good night."

Now it became obvious why Judge Malloy intentionally delayed the sentencing until late in the day. By the time all was said and done, the clock read 4:15, and it was a Friday before a holiday weekend. He had known what our next steps would be. We would file an appeal with the New York State Appellate Division, Second Department, located in Brooklyn, as well as a show cause order containing a provision releasing the defendant on bail pending resolution of the appeal. While it would take several hours to draft the appropriate papers for the appeal, it didn't matter. Not only was the appeals court closed on the weekends, but Monday was also Memorial Day. Thus, Judge Malloy believed he ensured that the doctor would remain in jail at least through Tuesday, if not Wednesday. He knew full well that his sentence was illegal and that the appellate division would reverse. Why he would behave this way, I had no idea.

Unfortunately for the judge, he was about to meet another warrior, our firm's founding partner, Melvyn Rubenstein. Mel started our firm twenty-one years ago. He had graduated from the University of Pennsylvania Law School with honors and immediately secured a position with the New York County District Attorney's Office headed by the legendary Frank S. Hogan. Within two years he was trying cases in the office's elite homicide bureau.

Four years later, Mel and his roommate from college, Steve Sorkin, started their firm in the basement of an office building across from the county courthouse, right next to the cafeteria. Not the best office space, but it was a start, and eight years later they occupied the entire fourth floor of a class A building a short walk to the courthouse. Almost every day, Mel or one or two of his criminal lawyers would be found in the courthouse. Their reputation as a top-notch criminal defense firm started to grow, and it was mainly due to Mel's work ethic and his philosophy for the firm: "Anyone could do good legal work. We do excellent legal work."

As soon as I left the courthouse, I called Mel from the phone I just had installed in my car—a perk of being named a junior partner. I was in Riverhead, fifty-five miles away from our office in Mineola, which would take about an hour to cover in the holiday rush hour. I gave Mel the facts and asked for help. He said he needed some time to come up with a plan, and he would call me back as soon as it was completed.

True to his word, thirty minutes later, the call came in. He would draw up the show-cause order and contact a law school classmate who was now an appellate division judge. I would dictate the affidavit that would accompany the order over the phone to my secretary, who would have a draft ready by the time I got to the office. Mel had also reached out to a very combative Olga Raphael to ascertain how much cash she could accumulate within the next two hours for use as bail. My last task was to reach out to Peter Spore to tell him that we were trying to get a court order signed by an appellate judge and to ask if he would be available for a conference call. Peter, knowing that Malloy's sentence was illegal, agreed to make himself available and gave me his pager number. We had the plan; now we had to make it work.

By the time I arrived at our office, Mel had set up a meeting with Appellate Judge Salvatore J. Maddie, who agreed to hear our emergency application. Judge Maddie was appalled that Judge Malloy would knowingly incarcerate a citizen on an illegal sentence. He told us to meet him at a restaurant where he was attending a bar association function.

Mel told me that Mrs. Raphael was able to get $5,000 in cash and would be waiting in her car at the restaurant. Once we got the order signed, she would accompany me to the county jail in Riverhead to bail out her husband.

Mel and I arrived at the Royal Manor restaurant about 9:00 p.m. Mel had arranged for us to use the manager's office. When Judge Maddie appeared, we got Spore on the line. As both the defense and prosecutor agreed that the Malloy sentence was illegal, the show cause order was signed along with the additional order that Dr. Raphael be released on $5,000 cash bail pending appeal. With the signed order in hand, I found Mrs. Raphael and got her into my car, and we were off on a fifty-five-mile trip to Riverhead during which she, thankfully, said not a word.

We got to the county jail at about 11:15 p.m. So far everything had gone according to plan, but by now you know things never go according to plan in the practice of criminal law.

The first thing we did when we arrived at the jail's parking lot was to double count the cash Mrs. Raphael had with her in a plain brown paper bag that apparently had been buried, as evidenced by the dirt that still clung to its outside.

Twenty $100 bills, forty $50 bills and fifty $20 bills added up to the $5,000 we needed.

We both signed a receipt I hastily drew up, and I was off to the jail's after-hours door. The exterior of the jail complex was brilliantly lit by floodlights that illuminated a sign instructing me how to pay a cash bail. I rang the bell on the side of the door and smiled for the camera that was recording my presence.

After a few minutes, I heard keys in the inside door lock and came face-to-face with a correction officer who stood more than six feet tall and weighed 300 pounds. I told the officer I was there to bail out Dr. Luis Raphael and presented the show cause order signed by Judge Maddie. I also advised him that I had $5,000 in cash for bail.

The officer reviewed the order and asked for my identification. He then said he was not familiar with such an order, and I would need to speak to the lieutenant on duty.

I was ushered inside the building and searched for weapons or drugs or other contraband. We then proceeded down the hallway to a door made of floor-to-ceiling bars. After about a minute, the door was opened by an unseen individual. As we walked another twenty feet down the corridor, the barred door behind us closed and a second opened in front of us.

Lieutenant Reeves—I read his name on his badge—waited for us. I reiterated the reason for my being there and showed the court order to him. Reeves took the order and disappeared into his office to call the watch commander. After a few minutes he reappeared, this time accompanied by two officers who appeared even larger than the first officer I had met.

The lieutenant stated in no uncertain terms that there was a strong possibility I could be charged with attempted prison break of an inmate because he had never seen an order like this before. Furthermore, he believed the order was a forgery because it lacked the seal of the appellate division, the possession of which was a separate crime. He told me it would be in my best interests to leave the jail immediately, or he would arrest me.

I tried to explain the situation to him again, but before I had a chance to say anything meaningful, the lieutenant ordered the two officers, "Please escort the counselor out of the jail, immediately."

The two officers escorted me vigorously but professionally to the door I had previously entered. Their attitude said, "And don't come back."

Midnight found me in the jail's parking lot attempting to answer Mrs. Raphael's question "Where is my husband?" I told her I needed to call Mel. He was awaiting my call and did not like what he heard.

"Boss, the jail won't accept Judge Maddie's order. They said it was a forgery as it doesn't have the seal of the New York State Appellate Division on it."

"Sit tight" were Mel's only words of consolation.

Not that Mrs. Raphael and I had a choice since not much goes on in Riverhead at noon much less at midnight.

While we sat in the parking lot, things were occurring at a rapid pace back in Mineola. As soon as I hung up with Mel, he called Judge Maddie. Apparently, Maddie had been sound asleep, and Mel let the phone ring at least fifteen times. A groggy, and perhaps a slightly hungover, judge begrudgingly picked up the phone.

"Mel, there is no such thing as an Appellate Division seal," he said.

Mel told him I was in the jail parking lot awaiting instructions. "Let me see what I can do," Maddie replied.

The more he woke up, the more annoyed he got. If he was up and getting aggravated, the same should be true for the warden of the jail. Thankfully, Maddie had his number.

"Thomas, this is Salvatore Maddie, and I got an urgent problem at your jail," he yelled at the still-sleepy warden. "How dare your officers fail to follow an order of an appellate division judge? I should hold them and you collectively in contempt of court. I want it resolved and resolved now!"

Back in the jail parking lot I debated with myself whether or not to ask Mrs. Raphael how she managed to get $5,000 in cash at 4:30 p.m. on a Friday. I was sure it would be an interesting story considering the dirt-encrusted brown paper bag. My wavering stopped with a call from Mel.

"Go back in and get Dr. Raphael."

My response was equally as short. "If I don't call you back in thirty minutes, you better come get me out of jail."

I had not imagined we could get this far in eight hours, but here we were. Mel had worked miracles so far, and I believed our warrior had one more left in him, so I walked to the door and rang the bell again. I had visions of officers opening the door with guns drawn and a pair of handcuffs waiting for me. I was pleasantly surprised when instead of being arrested, I was shown into a side office and offered a cup of coffee while a sergeant and Lieutenant Reeves double-counted the bail money and gave me a receipt.

Shortly thereafter, they gave me Dr. Raphael.

As I was walking the doctor back to my car, Mrs. Raphael ran towards him, and they embraced. The doctor thanked me for all I had done.

I told him don't thank me.
It was your wife, your wife.

Judge Malloy resentenced Dr. Rafael to three years' probation, this time without a special condition of jail. Ten months passed before the judge and I crossed paths again at a Suffolk County Bar Association dinner.

After dinner, a group of us were at the bar, and he walked up to me. We exchanged greetings, and he asked how Dr. Rafael was doing. I responded he was doing fine and was surprised that he recalled the doctor's name. Malloy suggested we move away from the crowded bar to a quiet corner. He told me that six months before the Rafael case, his wife of fifty-two years was diagnosed with stage three cancer. They then embarked on an odyssey visiting oncologists, radiologists, surgeons and chemotherapy specialists. At each visit, their appointment time came and went without being seen. On several occasions, the couple had to wait over an hour past the designated appointment. "I understand these folks are busy, but to have patients sit and wait to be seen, sometimes over an hour, gives you the feeling they just don't care about you. You're just their next case, but for you this is the biggest crisis you have faced in your life.

"Compassion is lacking in the medical community. They are great at treating disease but horrible treating people. After my wife passed, I vowed that the next time a doctor came before me, he would wait and wait just like they made us wait.

"Too bad it had to be your client, Gregg.

"*Capisce?*"

CHAPTER SEVEN

Who Can You Trust?

I had a number of cases over the years that made me wonder who you can trust. Here are three of them.

The Bank Trust Officer?

"Three nights ago, two agents from the FBI came to our home and started to ask us questions about our friend and former neighbor Reed Woodman. They asked if we invested or loaned money to Reed. When we said we did to the tune of about $600,000 over a three-year period, the agents gave us a subpoena for five years of our bank records and told us that we were both subjects of a bank embezzlement investigation and that we needed to get a lawyer."

That was how my partner Alex and I met Paul and Mary Ann Blanchard.

Paul and Mary Ann went on to tell us how they met Reed Woodman, their close relationship with him over twenty-plus years and the business dealings they had with him. But nothing they said gave Alex or me any idea why the FBI made them a target of an investigation.

"We did not do anything wrong," the clients insisted at least three times during the interview.

To be sure, Alex and I did what we usually do when we had two spouses, siblings or partners involved in investigation. We split them up for a one-on-one.

It would not be the first time one spouse knew of questionable activities that the other was oblivious to. Most of the time, the technique worked, but after an additional hour with the Blanchards, Alex and I believed they were innocent but naïve. The key to the investigation would be to find out, just how naïve were they?

The Federal Doctrine of Willful Blindness

In federal law legal speak, there are three categories a person can fall into during the course of an investigation. The first is a target, which means the government has substantial evidence to believe that the person has committed a crime. At the opposite end of the spectrum is a witness, a person who has information the government considers important to a criminal investigation but who has no criminal exposure or is only tangentially implicated. The last designation, a subject, falls in between. In layman's terms, a subject has at the very least engaged

> in suspicious conduct, and an investigation has commenced to determine if the subject has any criminal culpability that would move him to the target class.
>
> For a person to be found guilty of a crime, the government must prove beyond a reasonable doubt the defendant had the criminal intent to commit acts for which he is charged. However, the government can still obtain a conviction if it proves the defendant "consciously avoided" learning of the criminal facts. The doctrine, often referred to as Willful Blindness, "permits the jury to find a defendant has culpable knowledge of a fact when the evidence shows that they intentionally avoided confirming the facts."

Halfway through our separate interviews, Alex and I had a pretty good idea of what happened. However, the Blanchards did not have even a hint of any wrongdoing. We had to be sure they had no or very little criminal exposure before we would agree to an interview by the FBI. On the other hand, if the facts indicated they did have criminal exposure, we would immediately ask for a meeting with the assistant US attorney in charge of the case in hopes of obtaining immunity from prosecution for them in return for their full and truthful testimony against Woodman. Doing so is infinitely more complicated than it sounds.

After Alex and I had two more meetings with the Blanchards and examined the same bank records subpoenaed by the government, we concluded they had no criminal liability, unless you counted trusting an almost-family-member a crime. We opted for an informal interview with the FBI at their office to tell our side of the story. This is what transpired as Agent Mahan conducted Mr. Blanchard's interview.

Q: Mr. Blanchard, my name is Special Agent Jean Mahan, and this is my colleague Special Agent Debbie Moon. We are investigating certain activities of Reed Woodman in connection with an alleged embezzlement, which occurred at the Hamilton National Bank headquartered in Riverhead, New York. We understand that you have known Mr. Woodman for some time and had some financial dealings with him. It is those relationships that are the subject of our interview.

While we have agreed to your attorney's request that anything you say in this interview will not be used against you, I must advise you that if you lie in this interview, you can be prosecuted for the crime of obstruction of justice, which carries a maximum sentence of five years in a federal penitentiary. Do you understand that and are you willing to proceed?

A: Yes, I am.

Q: Why don't we start at the beginning and you tell us how you met Reed Woodman and came to give him money to invest?

A: Mary Ann and I met Reed and his then-wife Rhonda in March 1962. We both purchased new homes in the Saint James community of College Park, and we're next-door neighbors. At the time we were both newly married and developed a friendship. We became close friends. Since both our families live outside of New York, they became our extended family, and we often shared holidays, birthdays and anniversaries and even took several vacations together. In 1978, or there about, Reed and Rhonda divorced, and they sold their home next to ours. While we remained in contact, we saw less and less of each other over the years. Rhonda moved back to Pennsylvania to be closer to her parents, and Reed bought a home in the exclusive part of Saint James called Nissequogue, which overlooked Long Island Sound.

Q: What do you do for a living, Paul?

A: I am a carpenter by trade. I build fine cabinets and furniture and do general construction work on new homes and remodels. I now have my own business, Sound Framing, which employs six people.

Q: Do you know Reed's occupation and what he does?

A: He is a banker. Over the years, he has worked at several banks. He is currently a vice president or something like that at Hamilton National Bank. I believe his job is to bring new customers into the bank. He has connections with wealthy people on Long Island and in New York City, and with his Irish gift of gab, he is able to make them customers of the bank.

Q: Did there come a time when you gave Reed Woodman money to invest for you? And how did that occur?
A: Yes. In the summer of 1980, Reed invited Mary Ann and me to dinner at the Nissequogue Country Club. During that dinner, he told us that he was heading an investment group under the auspices of Hamilton Bank that provided bridge loans to various customers of the bank.
Q: Did he explain to you what a bridge loan was?
A: It sounded a bit complicated, but it basically was that companies needed short-term money during the time it took for the bank to complete the loan process. The company was going to get the loan; it just took time. That's what he called a bridge loan.
Q: What was Reed's role in the bridge loans?
A: The bank put him in charge of getting bridge loans for their customers. He would reach out to high-net-worth customers of the bank and offer them the opportunity to invest in the Bridge Loan Investment Program with the minimum investment of $500,000.
Q: Did you have $500,000 to invest?
A: Hell no. Reed knew we didn't have that kind of money. But he did tell us of an opportunity he was putting together where the bank would allow a group of friends and family to pool their money together in order to reach the minimum.
Q: Was Reed trying to sell you on the deal?
A: No. He is a close friend and was telling us about this because the program paid interest at a much

higher rate than you could get on a short-term CD from the bank, and he knew that we had two CDs at the bank for our two daughters' college funds.

Q: Did you ask if the bridge loan investment program was insured?

A: We sure did, and Reed said it was not. However, since the bridge loans would be paid back out of the loan the bank was in the process of completing and it would be the first disbursements from the loan, he said it was 98-percent safe. It was a pretty safe bet for a much higher interest rate.

Q: Did you invest any money with Reed in the bridge loan program?

A: After listening to Reed, in January 1981, we gave him $100,000 to invest for us.

Q: Where did you get the money from?

A: Neither Mary Ann nor I went to college, but we felt education was extremely important in this day and age. So, we diligently over the years saved money for our daughters to go to college. We had approximately $50,000 in each child's account, and we gave that amount to Reed.

Q: How did you physically make the investment?

A: As Reed was aggregating the money to make the $500,000 minimum, he asked that we make a check out payable to him.

Q: Did you not think it was strange to make your check payable to Reed personally?

A: You just don't understand. Reed is family. We trust him. For Christ's sake, Reed is godfather to both Cheryl Ann and Denise. He would never do anything to hurt those kids. They've been calling him "Uncle Reed" since they were able to talk. And as he doesn't have any children of his own, he's like their second father. Of course, we trusted him.

Q: Did you get this loan repaid and how?

A: Yes, we did. In July 1981, Reed gave us a check drawn on Hamilton Bank in the amount of $125,000.

Q: Is this the check? And how is it signed?

A: That is the check, and it's signed "Reed Woodman, Trust Officer."

Q: Do you think it was strange you got a check from the bank signed by Reed that paid that amount of interest in just six months?

A: No. Reed said that the bridge loan would be paid out from the bank's loan to the customer, and we got a Hamilton Bank check. Reed also told us that the interest was in line with other bridge loan rates across the country. Honestly, it was a good deal. We trusted Reed, and we got our money back plus good interest. We weren't interested in anything else.

Q: Did you make any other investments in Reed's investment group?

A: Yes. We made two other investments. The next one was in September 1981 when we took the $125,000 original investment and added another $125,000 from my IRA for a total of $250,000. This loan was paid back the same way in March 1982, and we got a return of our original $250,000 loan plus $62,000 in interest. The last investment was in November 1982 when we took the money made on the last two transactions, reinvested it and added $288,000 from Mary Ann's IRA, for a total of $600,000. That loan was paid back in June 1983, plus interest of $121,000. It was at this time that Reed told us that the Bridge Loan Investment Program had ended.

Q: What did you do with the $721,000 you received in June 1983?

A: The money and interest earned went back to the girls' college funds and to our IRAs.

Q: Did you ever give any of the money you received from Hamilton Bank to Reed Woodman or someone he directed?

A: Of course not.

Q: Have you ever gone to a casino located in Atlantic City? And how did you get there?

A: Yes, on two occasions. On both, we took the free bus that leaves from the Smithtown Diner at 8:00 a.m. on Thursdays and takes you to the Harrah's Casino. It's a great deal, and you'll even get ten dollars in quarters to play the slots.

Q: Have you ever gone to Atlantic City on a private airplane from Republic Airport that was paid for by Reed Woodman or a company he controls?

A: No.

Q: Have you ever been at a casino in Atlantic City or in Las Vegas, Nevada, with Reed Woodman?

A: No.

Q: Are you aware that Reed Woodman has outstanding gambling debts at casinos in New Jersey and in Las Vegas?

A: Absolutely not. The Reed Woodman I know is not a gambler.

Q: Has Reed Woodman ever asked for your help in paying off his gambling debts?
A: No.
Q: Do you have any bank accounts outside of the United States in your name, your wife's name or in your daughters' names?
A: No. All our bank accounts are in Hamilton Bank.
Q: Do you know what the trust officer of a bank does?
A: Not really.
Q: Do you know where Reed Woodman lives?
A: He moved to Nissequogue after the divorce, but then later he moved to Oyster Bay.
Q: Have you been to his new house in Oyster Bay?
A: No, we have not. Ever since the divorce we seem to be drifting further and further apart from Reed.
Q: Have you ever been to his apartment on Sutton Place in New York City?
A: Definitely not.
Q: Mr. Blanchard, your attorney gave us three letters marked Exhibits A, B and C. I ask you to take a look at these and tell us what they are.
A: The exhibits are letters we received from Reed Woodman in 1981, 1982 and 1983 on Hamilton National Bank stationery showing the interest we received from the bridge loan program. The purpose of the letters was to set forth the interest we received for tax purposes. Although you did not ask, the answer is yes, we paid taxes on the interest we received from the program.

With that question the interview of Paul Blanchard by the FBI was concluded.

Three weeks later, I received a telephone call from Special Agent Debbie Moon who told me that Reed Woodman was arrested that morning on a ten-count indictment charging conspiracy and embezzlement by a bank officer. Specifically, it was alleged that Woodman, who had amassed considerable gambling debts at casinos in Atlantic City and in Las Vegas, engaged in a scheme where he recruited four groups of individuals to invest in a bridge loan investment group that, in fact, did not exist. The money loaned by the unwitting individuals went directly into Woodman's pocket to pay for his gambling debts and his elaborate lifestyle. When it came time to return the money borrowed from these individuals, Woodman used his position as a trust officer to embezzle money from estates and trusts he was managing to repay his investors. All individuals who invested in Woodman's bridge loan fund, except for one, were deemed by the government to be witnesses and would be asked to testify at his trial. Against the weight of all this evidence, Reed Woodman entered a plea of guilty and was sentenced to four years in state prison.

Guess you can't even trust a trust officer.

A Dying Lady?

I turned on the TV to the local news promptly at 11:00 p.m. It was Wednesday, February 16, 1994—Ash Wednesday, in fact. There was my law partner Hal with a large ash cross on his forehead surrounded by reporters shouting questions. I am sure the priest who left his artistic cross on Hal's forehead never thought his handiwork would soon be seen not only on local TV but in all four of the local papers, *The New York Times*, *New York Daily News*, *New York Post* and *Long Island Newsday*.

The image of Hal circled by a bevy of TV microphones and reporters quickly cut to a video of Collins University Hospital and then to the scene of a twenty-year-old, handcuffed behind his back, being led out of his home by two detectives.

The TV anchor related the events of the day in a solemn voice. "This morning at about 5 a.m., Iqbal Choudhry, a hospital employee, allegedly entered the room of a thirty-year-old woman dying of cancer at the Collins University Hospital's hospice program and sexually assaulted her in her own hospital bed. The woman, who sources say has only days to live, identified Choudhry as her attacker, and he is now being held on a million dollars cash bail."

The next video clip showed Hal again, responding to reporters with one sentence. "The kid is innocent," he boldly told the residents of New York City.

The next morning Hal and I met to start crafting our plan to defend Iqbal, who was the nephew

CASES YOU CAN'T MAKE UP

of one of our physician clients. Because Hal was the former deputy chief of our county's sex crime unit, he took the lead in this case while I interviewed Iqbal and gathered background information from his family. Due to the publicity generated by the case, it was being fast-tracked by the New York County District Attorney's office, and Linda Payton, chief of the sex crime unit, decided to handle the case herself.

I drove to the Manhattan Detention Complex in lower New York, affectionately known as the Tombs, to speak to Iqbal. I quickly learned:

+ He was twenty years old and in the United States from Pakistan on a student visa to attend New York University as a freshman in its pre-med program.
+ As part of a work-study program at the university, he worked at Collins University Hospital as a janitor three nights a week, Tuesday, Wednesday and Saturday
+ While it was true he was assigned to clean the room where the alleged attack occurred, he repeated many times that he did not commit the crime and that he was telling me the truth.

Iqbal told me his job was to damp mop the corridors and the patient rooms. Each night he would be assigned a different floor to mop. On February 15, his shift started at midnight and lasted until 6 a.m. the next morning. He was assigned to the hospice wing for the first time and was told there were forty rooms that required his attention. Each room had a single bed and water station and measured approximately ten feet by ten feet with a private bathroom with a roll-in shower that measured four by five feet. Because all but two of the rooms were occupied, he followed the hospital standard protocol of knocking softly on the door before entering. He would then enter the room, leave the door open and make sure the patient was in the bed before he entered the bathroom to clean the floor. On his way out of the room, he would mop the floor as quietly as possible so as not to interrupt a patient's sleep.

All the patients appeared asleep except for the one in room 303. When he knocked on the door, he heard a weak voice saying to come in. He did so and announced the purpose of his visit. Following hospital protocol, he left the door open while he worked. He mopped the bathroom, and as he was backing out of the room, the patient started to speak to him. He could not tell if the patient was male or female because the patient wore some sort of cap and had covers pulled up to the neck. He did recall the patient's sad facial expression.

The patient said, in a rather weak voice, "I am dying. Would you pray with me?"

Iqbal did not know how to respond, so he just said yes.

The patient asked if he would close the door to ensure some privacy and then spent several minutes in prayer. Iqbal didn't understand the words but knew the language was Hebrew. The patient then asked what his religion was. He said he was a Muslim, and the patient asked that he say a Muslim prayer, which Iqbal did.

After ten or fifteen minutes, Iqbal left the room and closed the door behind him. The rest of the night was uneventful, and he clocked out at 6:15 a.m. He then went to his apartment for a few hours' sleep before his noon class. As he left his home, two detectives and two police officers approached him, asked for his name and arrested him. They told him he was charged with rape in the first degree and was advised of his rights. At the end of our discussion, Iqbal once again repeated that he was innocent and that what he told me had been the entire truth.

After my meeting with Iqbal, I called Hal from the road and relayed the above information. Hal then reached out to ADA Payton and requested copies of the hospital surveillance footage for the hospice wing. He also told her that Iqbal unequivocally denied any criminal conduct and related to Payton what we had been told by him. While she had a reputation of being a tough and excellent trial attorney, Payton also had the reputation of being a fair prosecutor, and that reputation permeated her sex crimes unit, which was considered a model for the nation.

When Hal asked for additional information about the case, Payton said that she would not discuss the case because it was an ongoing investigation, but she would provide a copy of the hospital surveillance tape and reach out to him when she would be able to discuss the case in detail.

Perhaps it was due to Hal's reputation as a former prosecutor or perhaps Payton would have done it anyway, but two days later on Friday, February 18, Hal received her call. She asked if they could meet that very afternoon to discuss the case because there were several developments. The meeting was set for four o'clock.

The first comment from Payton startled Hal. "My gut tells me there is something in this case that just doesn't fit. "While the hospital surveillance tape shows your client entered the victim's room and later closed the door in violation of hospital rules, he is observed exiting the room after seventeen minutes. There was nothing unusual in his appearance when he left the room, and the time frame agrees with what he told you occurred in the room."

It was the circumstances surrounding the attack that troubled her. The patient's room was in fact cleaned that night, something she would not expect if his intent was to commit a rape. There was an eighteen-minute delay between Iqbal leaving the room and the victim pressing the call button to report the rape. The hospital conducted a rape kit examination, and it showed no sperm present on the victim or the bed sheets, although it was possible he used a condom.

Furthermore, given the patient's frail, thin condition, one would have expected to see bruising on her thighs, but none was present. The victim told the police her attacker held her down by her shoulders while he violated her, but again no bruises, scratches or lacerations were noted on her shoulders.

Cases You Can't Make Up

There were scratches on both the victim's inner thighs, but the scratches were made in an upward motion towards the victim's chest as opposed to downward scratches usually noted in similar attacks.

There was no latent evidence under the victim's fingernails except for her own skin cells and blood that matched her type. Although it was several hours after the attack when Iqbal was arrested, there was no trace evidence found on his nails, body or the janitorial uniform seized from his hospital locker.

After giving Hal this detailed information, Payton said, "I want your permission to speak to your client one on one, with you being present, of course. I need to speak to him to assess if he's telling you guys the truth."

Hal and I conferred. We agreed it was worth taking the gamble. While anything Iqbal said to Payton and her investigator could be used against him, I felt confident he was telling the truth. Hal agreed. Payton contacted the warden at the Tombs, and a meeting was scheduled for 6:00 p.m. As a sign of good faith, we asked Payton to request the warden immediately place Iqbal in administrative segregation for his own safety. We had already requested that, but it had not been accomplished. The warden, knowing an order when he got one, quickly agreed.

Before they had a chance to leave the district attorney's office for the five-minute walk to the Tombs, Payton received an urgent call, after which she told Hal there was a change of plans. Instead of the jail, they were going to the hospital located on First

Avenue. It would usually be a thirty-minute drive, but thanks to lights and sirens of a police car, they made the trip in under fifteen minutes.

They made a beeline to the hospital room of Esther Horowitz. An individual who identified himself as Irvin Cohen, the rabbi of Esther's temple, met them at her door. He told them he had everything already on tape, then he rushed Hal and Payton into the room, saying "Esther doesn't have much time left."

At the bedside, Payton introduced herself as the assistant district attorney in charge of the case and Hal as Iqbal Choudhry's lawyer. Esther asked the rabbi to raise the head of her bed. She was having trouble breathing and was clearly at death's door. She was emaciated, pale and complained she was cold even though she was wrapped in many blankets. Payton asked if it was alright with her if they taped her comments, and she agreed. As Esther started, tears formed in her eyes. As she spoke, she paused often to draw a labored breath.

"On TV, they were talking about my case. Someone said the defendant would be lucky if he wasn't beaten to death by other inmates for raping me, a woman dying of cancer. I thought about that poor boy in prison for something he didn't do."

Esther paused to wipe the tears from her eyes. She took another shallow breath, her wheezing audible.

"All he did was show kindness to me by staying with me for a few minutes and praying. I am the sole support of my mother, father and my two children. I made up the story so my family could sue the hospital and be able to support themselves with me gone."

She mustered all her strength and looked at Payton directly. "I could not go through with it. He is innocent. Please tell him I'm sorry."

That night, Esther Horowitz died at 11:47 p.m.

Two hours later, Hal picked up Iqbal Choudhry from the Tombs and drove him to his uncle's house in Huntington.

A Fire Insurance Broker?

I have been to several crime scenes, but never one as nice as the bar of a high-class country club on the Long Island North Shore, known as the Gold Coast. There are many country clubs on Long Island, but only a few cater to the old money. They are frequented by white Anglo-Saxon Protestants, although recently the rare Irish, Italian or German member is begrudgingly admitted so their initiation fees can bolster a sagging treasury. While many would say that these clubs are not for them, for their members, they are home away from home. As you casually walk over to an empty chair at the bar, you can hear one member trying to out-brag his friends with golf scores or professional accomplishments.

One such location became the place where an ingenious scam was committed by a fellow who did not care how his actions would affect others. He perpetrated the crime because he was bored, and more importantly to him, just because he could. His grandfather, father and uncle (a state supreme court judge) had all been members of the club. Now it was Leland Hollingsworth's time.

Leland graduated with an honors MBA from the Wharton School of Business, but for the next three years, he wandered aimlessly from one job to another, not satisfied that any position could challenge his superior intellect (or so he told his father). Leland was unable to find his niche until his father, the managing partner of a national CPA firm, had enough of Leland's wanderings and pressured his golf buddy, the owner of a midsized insurance brokerage, to hire his indecisive son.

Fortunately, Leland liked being an insurance broker, and the use of his family's prestige at the club plus his gift for bullshit enabled him to grab a number of new clients at the club's bar. His standard approach was to start a conversation concerning the condition of the golf course or the presence of the less desirable *nouveaux riches* who had joined the club. Eventually, he would steer the conversation to insurance. Not the dreaded life insurance but the more practical property insurance. The pitch would go something like this. "I just spoke at a national insurance seminar, and one of my co-panelists mentioned that approximately 72 percent of all homeowners do not sufficiently ensure their homes for fire. Your home must be worth well north of 2.2 million dollars, but do you know what your fire insurance limit is? You really should check. Let me know if I can be of assistance."

Leland correctly predicted that his fellow club members, whether living in Garden City or on the North Shore overlooking the Long Island Sound, had fire policies written at least ten years before the spike in real estate prices and were clearly underinsured. Leland would then propose new coverage, and he also added a new twist.

"I should tell you that I am a full-service agent. I find the best rates from top-notch national insurance companies and completely manage your account. You only pay one bill by sending the premium to my firm and we do everything else. We monitor any changes in real estate prices and constantly search for better insurance rates. We could even hold the policies for you and handle all claims. In short, we do all the heavy lifting."

Leland was a great salesman. Club members signed up and recommended their friends to him. Leland's employer saw all the new business and promoted him to junior partner after only six months at the firm. Leland's dad, granddad and uncle were also proud of their new star.

As his prestige grew at the club, so did his book of business. Club members just had to be on the cutting edge of trends, from getting their heart calcium scores to having sleep apnea tests to having underinsured residences protected.

While the club members took advantage of Leland's offer, Leland also took advantage of them.

The scam was relatively simple in theory but complex in its execution and just challenging enough for Leland's brain power. It was premised on the actuarial analysis that the chance of a fire in a house in their area was much lower than the national average. Once a customer signed up, Leland would present him with an insurance quote from two or three of the top national insurance carriers. The customer—or mark—would select one and send Leland a check for the premium made out to his employer's brokerage company. The customer would also sign the power of attorney form giving Leland direct control over the account after being told, "You are much too busy and too important to spend your time and effort on fire insurance matters."

These pompous club members, who liked to deceive their fellow members with their importance, did not know that Leland was also deceiving them. It took a lot of work to pull off but became easy for a genius like Leland who had a photographic memory.

Here is how it worked in round numbers:

- Leland sells you a $2.2 million fire insurance policy for a premium of $3,400 a year.
- You send Leland's employer a check for $3,400 and you are covered as of August 15, 1991.
- Leland also sends you a form to fill out and mail to the carrier giving him power of attorney over the policy.
- On September 1, 1991, Leland contacts the insurance company as your attorney-in-fact and reduces the coverage liability limit to $50,000.

- On September 21, 1991, Leland gets a premium refund check from the carrier as your attorney-in-fact in the amount of $2,600, and he cashes it at his bank.
- On July 1, 1992, Leland writes the carrier increasing the liability limit back to $2.2 million effective August 15, 1992.
- On July 15, 1992, the carrier sends Leland a premium renewal bill for $3,500 for the $2.2 million coverage. Leland forwards the bill to the client. The client sends the premium to the insurance broker, and Leland pays the carrier.
- On September 1, 1992, Leland reduces the liability limit to $50,000.
- The beat goes on.

Thanks to his photographic memory and his Mensa membership, Leland was able to keep track of the renewal dates of the policies of forty-three clients and manipulate the coverage dates so he would receive the premium refund checks.

It wasn't that Leland needed the money; what he needed was the thrill.

This practice went on for three years until an unfortunate accident occurred. A client, attempting to make crêpe Suzette complete with flaming liqueur caused her kitchen to catch fire, inflicting extensive damage to the rear portion of her mansion.

Unfortunately for Leland, he was vacationing on Martha's Vineyard when this happened. The client panicked when Leland was not available to take her call and contacted the insurance carrier directly. She was advised that her home was only covered for $50,000 instead of the $2.2 million she believed it was.

The client was outraged because the damage to her home well exceeded $50,000, and she complained to both Leland's boss and the carrier. The owner of the firm did not have a clue as to what happened until the carrier produced documents showing the coverage changes Leland made.

The furious homeowner commenced a lawsuit against the brokerage firm and filed a complaint with the Nassau County District Attorney's Office. The equally furious owner of the brokerage firm took immediate action and fired Leland.

To prepare for the lawsuit, the owner of the brokerage firm retained the services of a forensic auditing firm to review each one of the fire policies written by Leland. They found premium changes in half of them. The audit results were turned over to the district attorney's office.

Leland's uncle, the former supreme court justice, was a friend of my law firm's senior partner. He knew of our firm's dedication in representing its clients and recommended we represent him. Leland was bored during our initial meeting and was more interested in the artwork on the walls of the main conference room than in discussing the several felonies he was charged with. He was unconcerned about being indicted and said he did not need a lawyer but could explain his actions to the DA by himself and get off with not even a fine. Nevertheless, he signed a retainer agreement because his father was paying the fee. The plan was to have the senior partner conduct all the negotiations in hopes of disposing of the case without having Leland go to jail. I, along with my senior associate, was tasked to prepare the case for trial in the event negotiations failed.

By this time, I had practiced criminal law for over twenty-five years and represented several white-collar criminals who stole millions of dollars, but had never met anybody like Leland. He had no contrition or concern for what he had done. Nor was he concerned about the damage he did to his family's reputation. The psychiatrists who evaluated him would say Leland exhibited the behavior of a narcissistic sociopath: "highly arrogant, sense of entitlement, grandiose sense of status, exploits others and lacks empathy." His only concern was to get out from under the criminal charges. In short, it was all about him.

Our senior partner conducted extensive negotiations with the district attorney's office that miraculously resulted in a plea deal. Leland would admit to one count of grand larceny fourth degree, a class E felony, make full and complete restitution to his victims, surrender his insurance broker's license and receive a sentence of five years' probation. As a sign of good faith prior to the sentencing, we had Leland place $100,000 in escrow to cover restitution for his victims. The restitution amount was calculated to be the amount of monies Leland collected by reducing the liability limits of his clients' policies. The judge presiding over this case, in an extraordinary burst of kindness, signed off on the deal and agreed to sentence Leland to five years' probation if he made full restitution and surrendered his broker's license.

Instead of being grateful for a minor miracle that kept him out of jail, the true Leland showed up at sentencing. My senior partner advised the court that all the individuals defrauded by Leland had received restitution except three who had left Nassau County with no forwarding address. The amount we could not return came to approximately $3,100.

After the sentence was imposed, Leland approached the assistant DA on the case and asked that the $3,100 be returned to him. The district attorney went ballistic, and we couldn't believe Leland had the gall to ask for the money.

That act confirmed to all of us that Leland truly was a narcissistic sociopath.

Too bad, Leland. No refund for you.

CHAPTER EIGHT

Need a License to Steal? Own a Hospital

The most fascinating and extensive fraud I ever prosecuted had its foundations poured in 1961, when I was only fourteen years old, by a Hungarian immigrant physician with the strange name of Bonaparte DeChambeau. The manner in which the doctor devised methods to steal— not only from the Medicaid program but his partners as well—was so ingenious that he should've been an architect rather than a doctor. This is that story.

Bonaparte DeChambeau had many loves in his life.

Unfortunately, the practice of medicine was not one of them. All the sadder because he had a medical degree from the Sorbonne University in Paris. Rather Dr. Bona (as he insisted he be called) was addicted to the worldly joys of money, power, money, women and more money. Squat and short like his imperial namesake, Dr. Bona came to the States not to cure human ills but to create an empire. This empire was to take shape in the then-very-rural community of Suffolk County known as Kings Landing. The location was appropriately named as Dr. Bona had the strong desire to be a king.

His empire took many years of planning and construction to come to fruition, but in March 1961, Dr. Bona cut the gold ribbon that opened the doors to Kings General Hospital, known as KGH.

While he abhorred the practice of medicine, Dr. Bona was a student of the business of medicine. He knew that for KGH to not only survive but to also be the mine out of which he would dig all the riches he wanted, he would have to ensure that the hospital put a lot of fannies in its beds. To ensure this occurred, Dr. Bona invited area physicians who usually sent their patients to hospitals in the adjoining county of Nassau or even New York City to become investors in KGH. Dr. Bona would own 60 percent of the hospital stock and let each of forty local physicians own 1 percent.

Local doctors lined up to participate because owning 1 percent of something was better than getting 100 percent of the nothing they got when they sent their patients to out of the area hospitals. It was truly a win-win situation. Patients won by being able to get quality medical care closer to their home, and the hospital owners won by being guaranteed a substantial return on their investment because they controlled the number of hospital admissions. When KGH opened, it boasted 110 medical and surgical beds, two operating rooms, a blood and pathology lab, a state-of-the-art radiology suite, an emergency department and a five-bed intensive care unit. There was nothing close to KGH in Suffolk County, and it would not be until 1980 that real competition would develop from University Hospital. A challenge that Dr. Bona would not have to face.

To reach his lofty goals, Bona realized he could not do it alone. He needed to establish a cabal by finding people to help him, people with certain expertise who were concerned with the welfare of the hospital's patients but also concerned about accumulation of their personal wealth. They could combine their separate talents to help Bona steal as much as he could. And of course, they would be rewarded.

His first choice for his corrupt inner circle was an obvious one—Luc DeChambeau, his nephew. Luc Dee, as he was professionally known—the family obviously had a problem with their last name—was working as an assistant administrator in charge of five departments at City Medical Center in New York when his uncle reached out to him. Luc was only thirty-two years old, tall, good-looking and the heart-throb of the ladies working in the hospital's billing office. In addition, he was bright and aggressive and had a great work ethic.

Dr. Bona wanted Luc to be the face of KGH, a role for which he was well-suited. He was always well-groomed, wore custom-made suits (as opposed to Dr. Bona, who could afford better but opted for off-the-rack suits with little or no tailoring) and spoke without

Bona's strong Hungarian accent. Luc's appearance rivaled that of the group of blue-blood hospital administrators from New York City who had great influence with the New York State Health Department. He also had traits known only to his uncle. Like all DeChambeaus, Luc had larceny in his heart and shared the DeChambeau family curse of greed. These were the exact traits Uncle Bona wanted in a chief executive officer for KGH, and he offered Luc the position as its administrator at double the salary he was making. When Luc expressed surprise at this salary offer, Uncle Bona told him that in addition to being a class A administrator, he would assist his uncle in special assignments that he would keep secret from the rest of the partners. The money did the trick, and Luc Dee accepted the position.

The first member of the cabal was now in place.

For his schemes to work to their fullest potential, Dr. Bona had to operate an outstanding hospital to avoid the scrutiny of the health department, and he did. To achieve his demand for a high quality of patient care, Bona knew he had to make sure the nursing care at the hospital was equal to, if not better than, the care patients received at the major New York City hospitals. As a community hospital, the bulk of the patient care at KGH was rendered by nurses. The admitting doctor only saw their patients for a few minutes each day during rounds. The rest of the time the nursing staff rendered care, monitored the patient's condition and notified the doctor of any change in the patient's status. Accordingly, Dr. Bona hired Melissa "Missy" Kean as KGH's director of nursing. Missy was not only a registered nurse but also had her doctorate in nursing from Stanford University. Prior to joining the KGH staff, Missy was the director of nursing at MD Anderson Cancer Center, part of the University of Texas. She also had a military air about her as evidenced by her rank of lieutenant commander in the US Navy Medical Reserve.

Dr. Bona first met the pretty red head with sharp green eyes when they were both students at the Sorbonne in Paris. In their younger days they were—to put it plainly—lovers. After graduation, they went their separate ways but always kept that last summer in Paris in their memories. Although Dr. Bona later married, he kept a very special place in his heart for his first love.

As the fates allowed, Dr. Bona and Missy would again meet twenty years later at a medical seminar at Johns Hopkins. Over the course of the five-day seminar, the night in Paris was relived. Dr. Bona knew that Missy had the brains and drive to run his new hospital's nursing staff and that, based upon their romantic relationship, she would keep secret that which needed to be kept secret.

When Dr. Bona made the offer to Missy to join KGH, she did not hesitate. Without knowing the full ramifications of what she was getting into, Missy joined the cabal.

The second member of the cabal was now secured.

Not yet knowing how to maximize KGH's potential for his own interests, Dr. Bona started small. He suggested to Luc that they (Luc) solicit a cash kickback from the representative of the surgical supply company that provided the hospital with very expensive, state-of-the-art, orthopedic implants. Luc came back, and told Dr. Bona that the salesman blew off a subtle request for a 10-percent kickback. He apologized to his uncle and said they had to continue to do business with the company because the orthopedic surgeons insisted on using its new proprietary implants.

But Luc did not fall far from the family tree. He did not reveal that the vendor actually agreed to pay a 5-percent kickback on the hospital's purchases, paid only to Luc.

Luc agreed ... Luc lied to his uncle and ... Luc pocketed the cash.

Luc believed he was due the extra cash because without him one of the largest cash cows for the cabal would not exist. While he was sure he would get his share of the illicit gains at year's end when Dr. Bona would whack up the cash, he also believed in the old adage about a bird in the hand.

What was Luc Dee's substantial contribution to the cabal, you ask? Well, it's rather complicated, but I'll do my best to explain the events.

When Luc reviewed the first three months of the hospital's operations, he found that the KGH lab was significantly underutilized. This initially proved to be a Catch-22 problem for him to solve. To be licensed by the state of New York, KGH had to maintain a fully staffed lab that provided blood analysis, pathology and X-rays. The problem was too many days when the hospital had too few patients needing lab services, and that translated into the lab having little work for its technicians. In short, the lab was losing money. Yet they had to have it per state regulation.

Luc arrived at a perfect solution to the problem and suggested to Uncle Bona that the lab be opened to outpatients, that is patients not admitted into the hospital but who were in need of the lab's service. It made perfect sense, so Bona agreed.

As often is the case with out-of-the-box thinking, the solution to the problem was successful and yet it spawned an unintended consequence. The consequence presented itself in the first month after the Outpatient Department Lab (always called the OPD) operation commenced and came to light from an unlikely source, namely the hospital's comptroller's office. Each Friday morning at eight, the comptroller's office would deliver three sealed money pouches to the administrator's office. Luc or his administrative assistant, Thomas Faulti, would double-check the count in each money bag, prepare a deposit ticket and deliver the bags to the armored car service on Friday afternoon for delivery to the hospital's bank for its weekly deposit.

This Friday morning, instead of having three money pouches delivered to the administrator's office, there were four. In addition to the usual pouches labeled Inpatient, Employee Cafeteria and Lab, there was a fourth labeled Outpatient Department Lab. The comptroller took it upon himself to break out the income generated by the new service..

Luc knew a gift horse when he saw one and immediately went to Uncle Bona to discuss the situation.

Once he got the information, Dr. Bona reached out to his second cousin Katlin Boral, the owner of the CPA firm that set up the hospital's accounting system. While she enjoyed the significant fees and prestige received from representing such a successful hospital, Katlin was always cautious of any interaction with Dr. Bona as he was always trying to push the legal limits. She was concerned about crossing the ethical line that would endanger both her accounting firm and her CPA license, so all the discussions she had with Dr. Bona were kept hypothetical. Thus, Katlin was extremely careful when she told Bona that when the accounting system was set up it did not anticipate OPD income as it did not exist at the inception of the hospital. Therefore, it was her suggestion that the OPD money be placed in the regular lab income funds or else OPD funds would, hypothetically, be considered off-the-books income. Dr. Bona immediately seized on the concept of off-the-books income and called for an emergency meeting of the cabal.

In that meeting Dr. Bona told Missy and Luc that the OPD income would not be deposited as income at the hospital. Instead, it would become income to their cabal. After all, Bona reasoned, the idea of maximizing the use of the lab was their idea, and there was no reason to share it with his forty partners.

When Luc asked how he should handle the funds that were in the OPD pouch, Dr. Bona came up with a quick solution. (Well, the solution was quick in Dr. Bona's mind, but it required a lot of work by Luc Dee.) Specifically, when Luc opened the money pouch from the OPD, he saw cash from the co-pays or direct payments from patients who used the lab's services, as well as some checks from various insurance companies. First, Luc would remove the cash from the pouch and set it aside. Then he would go to the checks. He was not able to have these checks cashed by the bank because they were payable to Kings General Hospital, so Dr. Bona told Luc to cash the checks himself. To do so, Luc would go to the cafeteria money pouch, which was almost all cash, and would take out cash equal to the total of the checks from the OPD pouch. For example, if the OPD pouch contained $3,455 in checks from insurance companies, Luc would remove $3,455 in cash from the cafeteria money pouch and replace it with the $3,455 worth of checks from the insurance companies. Thus, the cafeteria income would match the tally from the comptroller's office, but instead of being all in cash, it would now contain mostly, if not all, checks. Because the OPD income was off the books, no one would be the wiser.

All the cash was then given to Missy, who became the cabal's banker, and Dr. Bona had a wall safe installed in her office.

This system worked fine for several months, but then it started to take more and more of Luc's time to cash the OPD checks because the outpatient lab started to generate more and more business. He was now scouring the inpatient pouch trying to find additional cash. As Luc had other, more important work to do for the hospital, he enlisted his administrative assistant, Thomas Faulti, to come to his office every Friday and cash the checks. For his efforts, Luc gave Thomas $100 in cash for walking around money. As a twenty-six-year-old single male, Tom appreciated the extra money to use on the weekend.

The original three conspirators continued in their thievery, and significant dollars accumulated in Missy's safe until December 21 of each year when they would meet in Dr. Bona's estate overlooking Long Island Sound to divide up the money. Bona would preside and, without providing any accounting to his partners in crime, give each a large manila envelope stuffed with cash as a Christmas bonus, in addition to the one they received from the hospital.

The ever-greedy Bona kept looking for additional ways to enrich himself and that way occurred quite fortuitously at his family Christmas party in 1965. It was there Bona met his daughter-in-law's father, Mario Gazzola, for the first time. Mario was unable to attend his daughter's wedding some five years earlier because he was serving a sentence in the Butner Federal Correctional Complex in North Carolina for racketeering. To Bona, Mario was the missing piece of the cabal. None of the other members had the guts or personality to go out and grab the money he wanted. They were content to steal money in dribs and drabs, but with Mario on board Bona had the ability to grab the golden ring.

Mario Gazzola started his career as a cement truck driver for Colonial Sandstone, which provided much of the concrete for Manhattan skyscrapers. More importantly, at least in the mind of Bona, Mario was a business agent for the International Brotherhood of Teamsters, Local 262, the union that was headed by Jimmy Hoffa. (Yes, that Jimmy Hoffa.) The fact that Gazzola was a convicted felon was not considered a strike against him; rather Mario was just the right medicine the doctor needed.

This was confirmed when Dr. Bona found out that Mario was convicted of soliciting and taking bribes from nonunion tradesmen in order to get work at various New York construction sites that were to be staffed solely by union members. In addition, Mario's physical appearance was intimidating. Although he only stood five feet, seven inches tall, one look at his body told you he worked out extensively (not much else to do in the federal lockup). He had large, muscular arms, and they were always visible as he only wore short-sleeve shirts. Notwithstanding his appearance, Mario was crafty and intelligent, at least when it came to getting what he wanted.

With the final member of the cabal now in place, it was time to really steal.

Thanks to growing demand, the hospital added another fifty-five medical and surgical beds and two operating room suites in 1963. While it is true that a hospital's patient census varies month-to-month (for example, elective surgery tends to decrease around the winter holidays and summer vacation months of July and August), KGH maintained a steady and impressive 93-percent patient occupancy rate. When the census dropped below the 90-percent mark, Dr. Bona sent a memo to the other hospital owners and the next month's census would miraculously return to projected level. One percent of something really did the trick.

The same was true of the utilization rate of the ancillary lab and X-ray services. The forty physician-owners controlled not only admissions to the hospital but the use of these services as well. If there was any question whether a given patient could benefit from a KGH inpatient admission or outpatient services, the issue was resolved in the patient's (and hospital's) favor. Clearly, most of the hospital's physician-owners saw no downside in overtreating their patients and certainly understood that it meant more profit at year's end.

How Do Hospitals Make Money?

Today, hospitals bill insurance carriers and the poor souls who don't have any kind of insurance (euphemistically called private payers) using the standardized diagnostic codes to describe the patient's condition. The hospital is then paid a flat fee for the services it provides during the entire course of care it renders to the patient. So, if you had an appendectomy, the hospital would bill your insurance company for CPT Code 44950 and the hospital would get a predetermined fee. This is also called an "episode of care" or "pay for performance." If your hospital got paid $27,500 for your appendectomy and it could provide the care you need for $21,000, it made a $6,500 profit. That's why you are sent home two days after major heart surgery.

In the mid-1960s, the reimbursement system was the complete opposite. It was a fee-for-service model. More bluntly put, the more services your hospital and doctor performed for you, the more they would get paid. The longer you stayed in the hospital, the more the doctor and hospital could charge. This model could also be gamed. If a physician had an ownership share in the hospital, the extra day or two you spent hospitalized just to be sure ultimately rebounded to the benefit of the hospital and its owners.

During the first four years of its operation under the fee-for-service model, Kings General Hospital truly became a gold mine for Dr. Bona and his forty partners. Each year they all got a handsome check reflecting their share of on-the-books profit. Indeed, by year three each of the forty partners had recouped their initial investment and the rest was going to be pure profit.

Then came 1965 when Dr. Bona and his partners hit the Daily Double. In that year, President Johnson signed the Medicare and Medicaid Act. Before the act, hospitals had to provide emergency care to people who had little or no insurance, but they did so knowing they would not get paid.

Medicare provided all retired Americans sixty-five and older with Part A (hospital insurance) free of charge as part of their Social Security benefits and offered the retirees the opportunity to purchase Part B (physician coverage) for a small fee. In its first year of operation nineteen million people signed up for Medicare. In addition to medical coverage for the elderly, the act also created Medicaid, a joint federal-state program, which provided healthcare coverage for those who were deemed to be living below the poverty level.

From the KGH perspective, Medicare and Medicaid payments were like having the winning lottery ticket. Now those individuals the hospital treated at a loss or even free of charge as charity cases had government-sponsored insurance. Under the Medicare and Medicaid reimbursement formula, all the costs associated with treating elderly or indigent patients (subject to certain cost ceilings) plus a profit factor would be calculated and reimbursed to the hospital. The more it cost KGH to provide care to this class of patients, the more KGH would get in Medicare and Medicaid reimbursement.

As a result, in 1966, 24 percent of the patient stays at KGH were now being paid for by Medicare when the year before most of these cases would have resulted in losses or broken even at best.

Cha-ching! Cha-ching! Medicare and Medicaid money now started to fill the KGH coffers and ultimately the pockets of its partners.

Even in light of this good fortune, the greedy, very greedy Dr. Bona continued to gripe about his partners: "I pay their mortgages and country club dues. I made each of these peasants rich."

While there was some truth in Dr. Bona's statement, he conveniently forgot that without the other forty "peasants" and their enlightened self-interest to fill the beds and use the services at KGH, the hospital could pass for an abandoned Marriott Hotel. While Dr. Bona was living extremely well off the profits made at KGH as well as a small nursing home he owned in Queens, his addictive personality wanted more and more. To him, KGH was his creation and his private piggy bank, and because it was his piggy bank, he should get a bigger slice of the pie, even if it meant stealing from his forty partners. While he knew by stealing from his partners, he would also be stealing from Medicare and Medicaid, he cared not.

Scenes From a Criminal Lawyer's Notebook

In April 1966, the doctor and Mario concocted the plan that was to make Mario rich and Dr. Bona richer. The plan they came up with was quite simple and equally brilliant.

Mario would establish a C corporation owned 100 percent by him on paper but in truth was owned 80/20 with Dr. Bona. (Guess who got the 80 percent?) The corporation was to be called TIOM, their acronym for This Is Our Money. The initial purpose of TIOM was for it to become the linen and laundry supplier to KGH.

If you have been paying attention, you realize the hospital had been in business a little over five years and already had a linen supplier, Country One Linen. Moreover, for TIOM to get into the laundry business would require a substantial capital outlay that Bona refused to make. Instead of purchasing or renting a linen-processing facility; buying thousands of sheets, pillowcases and towels; hiring employees to process the linen and creating a fleet of trucks to deliver them, Mario would put his experience as a criminal to good use. The plan was simple. As they say in mob terms, Mario would muscle in on Country One Linen.

The discussion between Mario and Jeffery Myles, Country One's president, was short, but not so sweet. Myles was terrified as the gruff Gazzola gave him the choice of continuing to provide services to the hospital under the terms set forth or be totally excluded as the linen vendor. Mario demanded that Country One become a subcontractor for TIOM. It would charge TIOM 90 percent of its usual bill to the hospital. At the same time, TIOM would increase its bill for linen to the hospital by 10 percent. By paying 10 percent less and charging the hospital 10 percent more, TIOM would make a 20-percent profit on the KGH laundry bill while essentially doing nothing. Not wanting to lose his largest customer, Myles agreed to Mario's terms.

As Mario had expertise in making money out of nothing, the next step in the plan was to have TIOM become a general vendor to KGH. TIOM would become active in its own right and sell items like medical supplies, cleaning products, paper products and office supplies to the hospital in the designated amount of $235,056.31 in 1967 and then increase that amount by 15 percent each year.

The goal for TIOM sales to the hospital was easy to achieve because TIOM provided nothing to KGH. Providing nothing, however, is not easy. This portion of Mario's job required him to submit TIOM invoices to the hospital for the phantom goods. As no goods were provided, Mario also had to obtain the purchase orders and receiving documents used by the hospital from Luc. He then falsified purchase orders by forging the signature of various department heads and delivery tickets with signatures of people who worked in the hospital's receiving department.

The forged documents along with the TIOM invoice were given to Luc. Although unusual for an administrator to handle invoices and delivery documents, each month Luc would deliver a stack of TIOM invoices to the accounts payable supervisor for processing. The supervisor, who liked the very charming Luc, took the invoices he gave her for processing without thinking twice. "He was the boss," she would later explain. Moreover, the payment of around $19,500 a month to a vendor was not out of the ordinary for a hospital budget of several hundred thousand dollars a year.

Mario's business of selling nothing became such a success that he needed and was given a small office inside Missy Kean's office suite to work from.

When he got the checks payable to TIOM, Mario would go to his neighborhood bank (where he was well known and thought of as a good customer) and cash the KGH checks for TIOM's payroll. The bank obliged, and Mario took the cash to Missy, who placed it in her office's secret wall safe to which only she and Dr. Bona had the combination.

After listening to Dr. Bona drone on about how he made his partners rich, it occurred to Mario that Bona was also making vendors to the hospital rich. Always looking for an angle, Mario told Bona he had an idea for the vendors to share their good fortune with the cabal.

Since he was in the hospital almost every day, Mario noticed that several vendors of the same services regularly visited KGH. Initially, he noted that the hospital used three different meat vendors and set out to discover why this happened. His research uncovered that when the hospital first opened in March

1961, no single vendor wanted to have KGH run up a bill in the event the fledgling hospital went bankrupt. Therefore, Dr. Bona was forced to use several vendors to get the amount of supplies and credit he needed. But by 1966, the hospital had become an A++ credit risk and was still growing. To test out his theory, Mario set up a meeting with a supplier located in the meatpacking district of New York.

At the meeting, Mario presented a simple proposition, "You, Mr. Butcher have the opportunity to get all the hospital's business on the condition you pay me 5 percent of all the sales you make this year and then 10 percent of all your sales going forward in cash. Additionally, starting immediately, you will submit a fictitious invoice each month in the amount of $1,250 and bring me the cash when the hospital pays your bill. If you don't agree, you're out of here, *subito*."

To give Dr. Bona plausible deniability, it was agreed that all kickbacks would be asked for and paid to Mario without any indication the doctor was involved.

Mr. Butcher quickly agreed to Mario's terms. Capitalizing on his success, Mario, with the approval of Dr. Bona, expanded the kickback and phony invoice scam to include the grocer, dairyman, plumber and vendor of institutional supplies.

Exterminating Rats

The meeting with the butcher, and subsequently the other vendors, all took place in Gazzola's office located in Missy's suite. Because Mario had had a few run-ins with wiretaps or a recording device placed on a cooperating witness (who Gazzola, with much disdain in his voice, called a rat) during his union days, he knew that such recordings could be devastating and lead to another six-by-eight-foot cell. Accordingly, he took precautions. Eavesdropping to collect evidence required probable cause and a warrant signed by a judge. For that reason, Mario was confident there were no wiretaps on the hospital phones or in his office. His schemes were too new for all that. Still, he was concerned about a wired-up vendor.

The standard equipment used for such an undercover operation was called a Kell device. The device—enormous compared to today's microtechnology—was in a thin metal box measuring approximately two and a half by five inches that housed a small tape recorder and a radio transmitter. A microphone was then hidden in the undercover agent's clothing and everything said in the conversation was memorialized on the device's tape recorder. The transmitter sent a signal to a remote location where

> agents were listening in and also recording the radio feed. Gazzola told Dr. Bona about his concern, and to alleviate Mario's fears, Missy Kean's bottom desk drawer was equipped with a radio frequency scanner that would be turned on during a vendor meeting and monitored by Missy. Because the Kell device was always broadcasting a radio signal once it was placed on the informant's body, Mario always started the meeting with three to five minutes of innocuous small talk to give Missy sufficient time to scan all the radio frequencies. If all was clear, Missy triggered a light on Mario's phone, and the real purpose of the meeting commenced.
>
> Mario hated the spies and snitches he called rats and often told the story of one who was wearing the Kell device in the cup portion of a jock strap when the device malfunctioned and started to overheat, causing the informant to run out of a union meeting.
>
> "I hope he fried his balls off" was how Mario ended the story.

One conversation that unfortunately was not recorded occurred during the second meeting with the butcher, who went to Mario's office to pay his first 5-percent kickback and $1,250 more for the first batch of fictitious invoices sent to the hospital. According to the butcher, the conversation went something like this:

Mario: What kind of *stunod* (*Italian for* stupid) are you? This place is a hospital ... not Gallagher's Steakhouse! You don't serve rib roast, filet mignon or New York strip in a hospital! (*throwing the invoice back at the butcher*) Learn to do it right or I will personally throw you out of here forever!

The butcher would later testify he went back to his shop and redid the phony invoice as Mario directed.

Knowing that by paying off Mario they were assured continued business, the vendors started to cut corners to recoup the costs of the kickbacks. Mario did not care. Rather, he enjoyed his newfound power, and to curry the favor of his co-conspirators, he played Santa Claus.

When Missy Kean told Dr. Bona that she "just needed more space" at her Oyster Bay Cove home, he told Mario to handle it. After the construction of a three-room extension was completed by a construction company that did business with KGH, the contractor was told to bill the hospital for the work by means of a phony invoice stating that the work was done in the hospital's receiving department.

The contractor was also told to submit an estimate for the installation of an additional cesspool at the hospital in the amount of $60,000 when the job really cost $40,000. KGH paid the $60,000 to the contractor, who was told to pay the extra $20,000 to Mario in cash.

When Dr. Bona's central air conditioning failed, Mario came to the rescue. The hospital's HVAC contractor was told to install a brand-new system at Bona's home and bill the hospital for the entire job plus $2,000 in cash to Mario and an additional $1,000 for the Nurses Fund.

The Christmas list of presents continued, all paid for by KGH:

✦ KitchenAid dishwasher and Sub-Zero refrigerator for Luc.
✦ Air-conditioning unit and carpet for Missy's boat.
✦ A washer and dryer for Mario.
✦ A washer, alarm system and landscaping at Dr. Bona's house.

Multi-millionaire Bona even had two convex mirrors sent from Long Island to his winter home in Boca Raton, Florida, for a measly $300, which of course was billed to the hospital.

Dr. Bona observed how easy it was for Mario (who he deemed to be mentally and socially inferior to himself) to bring in money and decided he wanted in on the fun. Up until now, if the payoffs were ever detected, Dr. Bona could have hidden behind the rogue employee, Mario Gazzola, and be outraged by his self-dealing and thefts from KGH. However, being an egomaniac, Dr. Bona believed he could do much better than Mario so he came out of the shadow.

It was then that the money-hungry Dr. Bona started his own private bank. From time to time, vendors to the hospital would have cash-flow problems and approach the wealthy Dr. Bona for a loan. If a vendor needed a $50,000 loan, he would speak to Dr.

Bona, expecting that the doctor himself would loan him the funds. Wrong. The vendor was told to submit two $25,000 phony invoices to the hospital, and Bona would make sure the hospital paid them. Six months thereafter when the loan was due, it was paid (interestingly without interest) in cash directly to Dr. Bona. What a deal! At least three vendors took advantage of the interest-free loans from the Bank of Bona.

The sadistic thrill of having power over his vendors was never better illustrated than by Dr. Bona's personal shakedown of the old guy who ran the café at the hospital. Breakfast and lunch were served seven days a week for hospital visitors and staff. According to the contract between the hospital and the café, the monthly rent to the hospital was $1,250 for a term of five years. At the contract signing, Dr. Bona pulled the café owner aside and told him the real rent was $1,550 per month and that Bona expected the $300 difference to be paid in cash directly to him each month. So, on or about the first of each month Dr. Bona would go to the café as soon as he got to the hospital and wish the owner, "Good morning, my dear friend."

That was the owner's cue to assemble $300 in cash and place it in an envelope. Sometime that afternoon, Dr. Bona would come into the café, wave to the owner and proceed to the men's room. The old man would then get the envelope, enter the men's room, use the urinal next to Bona's and pass him the envelope as each man peed.

Ah, the thrill of committing a crime in person!

Clearly, Dr. Bona had orchestrated a criminal enterprise to steal from his forty partners. The cash stolen via the OPD, the kickbacks and the paid fictitious invoices all found their way into Missy's office safe and over the years counted in the millions. This amount did not include the personal items the hospital paid for that went to the members of the cabal.

Dr. Bona simultaneously stole from the New York State taxpayers. Under the New York State Medicaid Program, each hospital was given a separate reimbursement rate for the treatment of Medicaid patients. As you previously learned, a hospital's reimbursement rate was based on the costs incurred by the hospital for Medicaid patients divided by the number of days Medicaid patients spend in the hospital plus a profit factor to arrive at a daily rate. By inflating costs incurred and failing to offset certain costs with the income that a cost center generated, the fraudulent cost report KGH submitted caused the state to issue a Medicaid rate that was significantly higher than KGH should have been entitled.

How then was the KGH criminal enterprise discovered and prosecuted?

The answer is the same as with all major financial frauds, through a lot of hard work and a little good luck. And that's exactly what happened in the KGH case.

In early 1975, the three major New York newspapers

reported allegations of financial fraud and patient abuse in New York City's nursing home industry. The public was outraged by these reports, and Governor Hugh Carey responded by appointing Charles "Joe" Hynes to head the Office of the Special Prosecutor for Nursing Home Fraud.

Within a matter of months, the special prosecutor opened seven regional offices throughout the state. One was the Long Island Region, which had responsibility for Queens, Nassau and Suffolk Counties. I joined that fledgling office in July 1976 and was appointed a special assistant attorney general. The office we started was different than other prosecutors' offices. As the former chief of the Brooklyn Rackets Bureau, Hynes realized that if you placed a prosecutors, auditors and investigators in one office all working on the same case, a quicker and better investigation could be conducted, and if any crimes were discovered, a more efficient prosecution could follow. We did not know it then, but our team concept would prove so successful that it became the model for all the Medicaid fraud offices that would in years to come spring up over the country.

As a special assistant attorney general, I headed up several teams of auditors and investigators. Our work resulted in several successful prosecutions of nursing homeowners and administrators.

One case I investigated resulted in the indictment and conviction of the majority owner of a small Queens County nursing home who accepted kickbacks from various vendors. It wasn't a large case, but it gave us a large lead. We found out this owner had a brother who was the majority owner of a nursing home in Nassau County. A review of that nursing home's vendor list showed the same vendors who paid kickbacks to the Queens home. That led to the indictment and conviction of the owner of the Nassau nursing home. The brothers were named Paul and Peter DeChambeau.

We learned Paul and Peter's father, Bonaparte, was the minority owner of both nursing homes and was the majority owner of Kings General Hospital. When the vendors who paid kickbacks to Paul and Peter testified in the grand jury, we also asked if they paid kickbacks to Dr. Bona or anyone at KGH.

The vendors were reluctant to testify because they were afraid of losing the KGH business, so when we asked about any kickbacks paid at the hospital, they, on the advice of their attorneys, refused to answer on the grounds that the special prosecutor's office lacked jurisdiction to prosecute hospitals. And they were right.

To make sure we were on the right track, our auditors reviewed the cost reports filed by KGH and compared them to cost reports filed by similar hospitals in our region. We found that costs incurred by KGH were significantly higher than its peers. That information coupled with the hospital's relationships with vendors who admitted paying kickbacks to nursing home administrators was sufficient to permit the governor to extend the jurisdiction of our office to one hospital: KGH.

We contacted KGH with a request for an audit. Well, the request was not really a request, because the invitation came via a grand jury subpoena, which would guarantee our office access to the original books and records of the hospital.

Once subpoenaed, the hospital had a choice. They could deliver five years of accounting ledgers, invoices, receiving documents and other accounting data to our office; or we could do the audit on-site so the hospital would not incur the costs of transporting the records to our office and we would have the records available as needed. (Remember, this case took place before the advent of electronic records.)

Our preference was to perform the audit on-site because we could have immediate access to employees of the hospital to explain certain transactions.

Our auditors were much more than your typical tick-and-tie accountants, who just make sure all the numbers are verified and the credits and debits balance. They were trained in forensic auditing techniques and would often accompany the investigators on interviews as needed. Also, because they worked in the same office as former police investigators and prosecutors, they learned many of the investigative techniques through osmosis, including the very basic "keep your ears open and your mouth shut."

While on site at the hospital every business day, sometimes for four to six weeks, the auditors would build a rapport with the hospital staff, most of whom were basically hard-working, honest people. These relationships would serve us well if the case proceeded to the indictment stage and we needed them to testify.

The downside of doing an audit on-site was that most institutions, be it a nursing home or a hospital, intentionally made things as difficult as possible for our staff. In the summer the audit site would be in an un-air-conditioned attic, while in winter the site would be in the basement of the hospital near the loading dock that was open most of the day. While at times the audit sites were challenging, the auditors persevered and did their job to the highest standard.

And so began the audit at KGH in 1981. It started in January, and as we suspected, the auditors were sequestered in a twelve-foot square room adjacent to a loading dock, which was not heated. Veronica "Ronnie" Rawlings, the office's associate chief auditor, was chosen to supervise the four-person audit team. I selected Rawlings to lead our team because I had worked with her on several nursing home audits and found that not only was she a superior auditor, she was also a damned good investigator. Ronnie possessed something else that most auditors did not have—street smarts. While the majority of our auditors came to the office directly out of college, Ronnie took a different path. After a rather rough childhood, she graduated high school and joined the navy. On discharge, she decided to go to college to study accounting. Her sixth sense for sniffing out criminal conduct would be part of the luck we had in this case.

By being on site at KGH every day, Rawlings took note of the slew of hospital pages that seemed to be announced constantly over the loudspeaker. The barrage in the morning got to be so annoying, one of the audit team suggested the speaker directly outside their makeshift office be disconnected. While some of the auditors just tuned out the pages in favor of the jazz music being played on the radio and others just ignored them, Ronnie did not. "Dr. Matthias dial 341," "Dr. Park to the ER" and "Code Blue, 3 South" seemed normal enough, but then Ronnie noted a pattern. Several times each day, a page would call: "Mr. Gazzola dial 678," or "Mr. Gazzola to receiving" or "Mr. Gazzola to administration."

She began to wonder, who is this Mr. Gazzola? She checked the hospital roster of employees, payroll records, the vendor list and even the attending doctors list ... no Mr. Gazzola.

That is when lady luck smiled on us. Trial lawyers define "luck" as preparation meeting opportunity. Ronnie's experience and preparation for this audit met the opportunity of paying attention to the inordinate number of pages for Mr. Gazzola, and we got our first break.

Because most of the pages for Gazzola had something to do with the receiving department, Ronnie decided to sit in on an interview one of the junior auditors was conducting with the head of receiving. While the junior auditor asked general audit program questions on the flow of paperwork and the department's procedure for checking in supplies delivered, Ronnie in an almost off-the-cuff manner asked whether Mr. Gazzola was part of the receiving department. To her surprise, the response was an emphatic no. Not ready to accept that short answer, Rawlings followed up, "Well, he must be important with all the pages he gets every day."

The response came, "Yeah, I guess so. He is somehow related to Dr. Bona and owns TIOM."

Ronnie left the answer as given and let her colleague proceed with his questioning. As soon as they both left the meeting, Rawlings was pouring over the vendor list, and lo and behold, she found that TIOM was a major hospital vendor. TIOM first showed up as a KGH vendor in late 1966 and replaced the hospital's original linen vendor, Country One Linen. She noted that in 1967 TIOM billed the hospital $277,000, and that amount escalated to $331,500 in 1970, a higher rate of yearly increase than Country One had been charging.

Ronnie then contacted the lead investigator on the case, John Sterno, to see what he could find out about Mr. Gazzola. Within two days John found out that Mario Gazzola was the father-in-law of Dr. Bona's youngest son; had three arrests in New York, with one culminating in a misdemeanor assault conviction; and had served five years in federal prison for racketeering. John then turned his attention to TIOM and gathered the incorporation documents that showed it was formed in 1967 and that Mario Gazzola was its sole owner. In another three days' time, John, using information obtained from his former colleagues at the FBI, was able to get enough background on Mario's union activities that made him a person we desperately wanted to interview. All this without the benefit of the Internet.

However, before we interviewed Mario, we wanted to get more information on TIOM and decided the best place to start was with the linen vendor it replaced at the hospital. Accordingly, Sterno, along with Rawlings, decided to pay an unannounced visit to Jeffery Myles, the owner of Country One. When they met Mr. Myles at his office, he was initially cordial. It was only after the investigators told him they were investigating KGH in general and Mr. Gazzola in particular that his attitude changed 180 degrees. Upon mention of Mr. Gazzola's name, Myles became agitated and then downright belligerent. He ordered the investigators out of his office immediately and in the course thereof he made it very (expletives deleted) clear that he did not want to speak to them or any investigators from the Special Prosecutors Office. He also refused to give the investigators the name of his attorney.

Clearly, something was terribly wrong, and the only way we were going to get his attention was to issue Mr. Myles a grand jury subpoena. Which we did.

The subpoena served upon Mr. Myles did, in fact, get his attention, and the next thing we knew an attorney called and advised us that he was representing Myles in this matter. When we asked the attorney if he was willing to bring Mr. Myles into our office to be interviewed prior to his grand jury testimony, counsel told us his client was not willing to cooperate with us, but he would be truthful before the grand jury.

The heavy lifting on this grand jury investigation was left to our regional director, Rick Muffin. Rick was a career prosecutor spending thirteen years in the Manhattan District Attorney's Office run by the legendary Frank S. Hogan. While Rawlings did the background work on suspect vendors, I handled the grand jury presentation in order to get vendor records identified and placed in evidence. I also conducted the examination of some of the tangential witnesses. But the bulk of the work was to be done by Rick, and we were very fortunate that based on his experience in investigating and trying financial fraud cases, he was a quick study.

Three days before a scheduled grand jury presentation, Ronnie and I brought Rick up to speed and had all the grand jury exhibits marked for his review. Rick never disappointed, and by the time he finished a four-hour grand jury session with Mr. Myles, the difficult and at times obstinate witness told Rick how his firm was replaced at the hospital and about the deal he had to make with Mario Gazzola. As Myles told Rick, "Having part of a customer is better than having no customer at all."

Now that we had an insight into the TIOM-Country One linen deal, the old adage that a leopard never changes his spots caused us to look deeper into Gazzola. As we spoke to the other major hospital vendors that Rawlings deemed suspicious, Gazzola's name kept popping up. It was obvious that these vendors hated the way they were treated by him, and when faced with either telling the truth before the grand jury or personally facing a perjury indictment, most of these vendors told the truth regarding Gazzola's shakedowns.

What Goes Around... Comes Around.

Earlier, I told you about the butcher and his run-in with Mario Gazzola over the fictitious order for filet mignon and other expensive cuts of meat. Mario made the butcher so paranoid that in order to keep track of the fictitious invoices he sent to KGH, the butcher started to place a star next to each fictitious invoice in his sales journal. The system not only helped the butcher keep track of the fictitious invoices and the money he had to pay to Mario, it also served as a roadmap for our audit staff to follow.

Thank you, Mr. Butcher

Other vendors also testified about the conversations with and payoffs to Gazzola, but none had any information directly linking Dr. Bona to these crimes. Without that testimony, we were sure Dr. Bona would say Gazzola was a disloyal family member and a rogue he should never have hired knowing about his criminal record. We were confident Dr. Bona would hang Mario out to dry and maybe send him a box of cookies each Christmas while he dined at an exclusive New York restaurant and Mario sat in his Sing Sing cell. We felt this could happen because the amount of kickbacks and fraudulent invoices we could lay at Mario's feet was fast approaching $895,000, and the audits and subpoenas for other vendors were still pending.

As the investigation into Gazzola's shakedown of the vendors intensified and more of the vendors were being called into the grand jury, Rick got a call from a well-known New York City attorney who specialized in white collar crime. He told Rick that he had been hired by Gazzola and requested a meeting to discuss our investigation.

The meeting held in our office was more like two teams at the Super Bowl feeling each other out in the first quarter. The discussion started with Rick demanding Gazzola plead guilty to larceny and fully and truthfully cooperate with our investigation into KGH, Dr. Bona and any other officials at the hospital. In return we would ask the judge to sentence Gazzola to no more than three years in prison.

Rick suggested this was a rather generous offer because Gazzola was looking at fifteen years in jail. Mario's lawyer respectfully declined our generous offer and countered with a proposal that Mario would testify truthfully and fully cooperate with our investigation into Dr. Bona on one condition: "Mario gets a walk," or to put it more succinctly, he would not be prosecuted.

Both sides knew full well that Dr. Bona was the real target of the investigation, and each had a significant decision to make. Did Mario Gazzola push the envelope to see if we would indict and prosecute him for felony larceny, where he would be looking at significant jail time upon conviction? Did we look to shorten the investigation into Dr. Bona by making a deal with the devil? We also realized that Bona's attorney would have a field day cross examining Mario about all his criminal activities and that he was lying to escape punishment for his crimes if he testified against Dr. Bona. Could we save him by finding other evidence that would prove Mario was telling the truth?

All these and a multitude of other questions had to be answered before a decision could be made. To facilitate the decision, Rick asked Gazzola's attorney for an offer of proof as to Dr. Bona's involvement. In response, counsel gave a hypothetical. "Assuming Mario was given full immunity, he could tell you ..."

Armed with this information, Rick had a series of discussions with the New York City office brass, including Deputy Attorney General Hynes. While Rick was doing that, our audit and investigative staff ran down some of the leads given by Mario as tokens of good faith, all of which checked out. Accordingly, it was determined that Mario was telling us the truth.

And the guy who hated rats became what he hated the most to save his own skin. Mario knew full well Dr. Bona always looked down on him, thought he was expendable, and would turn on him in a minute. So, Mario Gazzola fired the kill shot first and got his immunity from prosecution.

Thanks to Gazzola the list of vendors who paid kickbacks and/or submitted phony invoices grew and grew and the grand jury was kept busy. The grand jurors nearly fell out of their chairs as Rick took Mario through his conversations with Dr. Bona and Missy; the shakedown of the vendors; the creation of the phony invoice scheme; the wall safe in Missy's office and that TIOM was an acronym that stood for This Is Our Money.

While some of the grand jurors were clearly annoyed with us for allowing a lowlife like Gazzola to escape criminal charges, they also understood that his testimony was critical to making the case against Dr. Bona. During his testimony, Gazzola was asked about the hospital administrator Luc Dee. Gazzola felt that Luc "definitely knew what was going on and most likely had a role in getting the phony invoices paid" but had no solid evidence to support his opinion. Luc rarely dealt with Mario and had the attitude that he was better than Mario and even better than Dr. Bona as he was starting to gain status and a reputation throughout the state's hospital community.

Young, handsome and a family man with three children, Luc had rapidly ascended the social ladder not only in the Kings Landing community but in New York State as well. Even the New York State Hospital Administrators Association dubbed Luc a boy wonder as he took a new hospital from the ground to great heights. Mario reiterated several times that he hated "the punk's condescending attitude" but could not say that Luc was involved or even knew about any of the scams. He did tell us, however, that Luc and his assistant, Thomas Faulti, would spend a lot of time in Luc's office every Friday doing something "which he had no knowledge of" but "looked very suspicious."

On the Wednesday before Easter, the grand jury had another session, which I was conducting, and six witnesses were scheduled to appear. The first witness was Margie Phillips, the hospital's business office manager, who gave us background information on the operation of that office. The next witnesses were vendors who were ordered to produce their records to the grand jury, and the last witness was Thomas Faulti. Because we had nothing specific to confront this witness with, I asked him for background information. I wanted his answers on the record.

Thomas told us he was a graduate of Queens College and had a degree in business management. He wished to become a hospital administrator in the future and was currently working as the assistant to Luc Dee at KGH. I asked whether he had any knowledge of any criminal wrongdoing at KGH. In response, Faulti said no on two separate occasions.

On the Monday after Easter, my phone rang promptly at eight o'clock in the morning, and it was Margie Phillips, my witness from the previous Wednesday. Margie was clearly upset. She started rambling about how she and her family were devout Baptists, tithed to the church, attended Wednesday Bible study and pledged to the Lord to do right. I did not know where she was going in her ramblings but let her continue. She told me that during the Easter service she discovered her nephew had sinned, and I needed to see him right away. I suggested that perhaps her pastor would be a better person to address the situation than I. She replied. "He certainly would be, except my nephew's name is Tommy Faulti."

Margie now had my full attention, and she agreed to bring Faulti in that evening. I notified Rawlings as well as the chief investigator, Anthony Josephs, to be on call as soon as they arrived.

At about 6:30, Margie and Tommy, as he was called by the family, came into my office. As I started the meeting, Tommy interrupted and said he wanted to get his issues off his "soul and conscience" immediately. While Tommy presented as a contrite sinner, I had to warn him that if his statements today differed from his grand jury testimony given under oath, he could be charged with the crime of perjury. However, if he gave us the truth today, I would agree not to proceed with a criminal case against him.

That seemed to relax Tommy, and over the next two hours he opened the door to the administrator's office and told us of how each Friday, he and Luc would exchange the OPD checks with cash from the cafeteria pouch. To corroborate Tommy's testimony, Rawlings did a quick review of the KGH bank deposits. That's exactly what most auditors would do, but Ronnie went a step further and looked at the deposit tickets themselves. They showed most of the deposits from the cafeteria were inexplicably made up entirely of checks. There would be other evidence to corroborate Tommy's testimony, but now we had a direct witness identifying Luc Dee as a member of the cabal.

The grand jury, after hearing all the evidence, had no difficulty in returning indictments against Bonaparte DeChambeau, Melissa Kean and Luc DeChambeau. The special prosecutor's office only had jurisdiction to charge thefts from the Medicaid program and conspiracy to defraud Medicaid to wit: these individuals worked together to inflate patient costs by submitting fictitious invoices, taking kickbacks and failing to report the outpatient department income. All these illegal activities ultimately resulted in the state of New York paying a higher Medicaid reimbursement rate to KGH than it had been entitled to.

The prosecution of the gang of three for theft from the other hospital partners had to be left to the local district attorney and the civil courts.

The evidence against all three defendants was overwhelming, and after nine to twelve months of making motions, which challenged our jurisdiction as well as the indictment itself, plea negotiations started.

Missy was the first defendant to plead guilty to Medicaid fraud, and she was sentenced to five years' probation.

Luc followed and was sentenced to one year of weekends in the Suffolk County Jail, commencing Friday at 6 p.m. and ending Monday at 6 a.m. He served about five months of his sentence before being admitted to Sloan Kettering Hospital, where he died of an aggressive form of cancer.

Dr. Bona was offered a plea deal whereby he would make full restitution to the Medicaid program plus interest and serve four years in a state prison. He rejected the offer and, being a con man to the end, blamed Luc and Gazzola for the crimes.

Unfortunately for us, the judge assigned to the case was a Suffolk County Supreme Court justice who had jurisdiction to hear both criminal and civil cases. The judge, called "the Vampire" by all those who appeared before him because he kept his courtroom dimly lit and at sixty-eight degrees no matter what the season, did not believe the case against Bona was a criminal case warranting jail time. As can be seen from the light sentences handed down to Missy and Luc, the judge believed that Medicaid fraud was a civil matter. He told us that if we convicted Dr. Bona after a trial or even if he took a plea to all the felonies in the indictment against him, he would not commit to a jail sentence. Rather, the sentence would be strictly up to him and he would hold a hearing on the issue.

Subsequently, Bona did plead to grand larceny, and the hearing insisted upon by the judge was held.

At the sentencing hearing, we reminded the judge of the facts we would have brought out at trial: the muscling in of Country One; the creation of TIOM; the demand for kickbacks from a multitude of hospital vendors; the demand that certain vendors issue fictitious invoices to the hospital; and the theft of the outpatient department income.

Following the judge's lead, defense counsel argued the case was strictly a financial one and that no patient harm had been alleged. Counsel also noted that Dr. Bona was prepared to make full restitution to the Medicaid program plus interest prior to being sentenced.

While these two factors appeared to have the judge leaning in Dr. Bona's favor, it was Bona's medical history that turned out to be the deciding factor. Bona called two witnesses at the hearing. His primary care physician stated that Dr. Bona was seventy-eight years old and suffered from a number of conditions, including kidney and cardiac issues. Concerning the kidney issue, Dr. Sean Kyle stated that every two to three months Dr. Bona's urethra contracted to the point where he was unable to pass urine. When that condition occurred, Bona had to go to a urologist who would then dilate his urethra. Not only was this procedure painful, it had to be done in a sterile environment such as an operating room. Performing the procedure in any other type of environment could introduce bacteria that could lead to a fatal case of sepsis. The doctor also opined that he was not aware of any such facilities in the state prison system and that at least every two to three months Dr. Bona would need to be transported to a hospital for the procedure.

His last witness was Dr. Jake Ryan, a noted cardiologist from Columbia University Hospital. Dr. Ryan's subspecialty was interventional cardiology, and he was considered the expert in the disease of aortic dissection. Dr. Ryan advised the court that he had examined Dr. Bona and determined that his aorta, the largest blood vessel branching off the heart, was abnormally distended. Due to Dr. Bona's high blood pressure, hardening of the arteries and a previous history of syphilis, there was a weakening or bulging in his ascending aorta. Dr. Ryan felt this patient's condition was perilous because his aorta had ballooned by 65 percent of its normal diameter. If the aorta ruptured and emergency heart surgery was not performed, the patient would die. Moreover, owing to Dr. Bona's age and physical condition, preemptive surgical repair of the aorta was not recommended because it was too dangerous. Dr. Ryan concluded that if Dr. Bona was sent to jail the stress would exacerbate his condition and that he would not be able to receive the type of medical care he required.

The judge than asked Dr. Ryan how long Dr. Bona had to live. After a long pause, the doctor said, "six to eight months, at best." This was in the summer of 1984.

The judge, who again stated that this was a civil case, accepted these medical findings hook, line and sinker. He sentenced Dr. Bona to make full and complete restitution to the state of New York and then placed him on five years' probation.

Four Years Later

I was called as a witness in a lawsuit filed by the State of New York Tax Department against Dr. Bona. Surprisingly (at least, I am sure, to Dr. Ryan), Dr. Bona was alive and well and still fighting with the state of New York over failing to report his illegal income.

After I testified, there was a break in the proceedings, and I walked out of the courtroom. As I opened the door to exit, Bonaparte DeChambeau himself was standing in front of me. I could have walked right by him without saying anything, but for some reason once I was face-to-face with him, I extended my hand and said, "Dr. Bona, my name is Gregg Naclerio."

Dr. Bona looked up at me, extended his stubby index finger, wagged it at me and said in his heavily accented English, "You ... I remember."

I remember you too, Doc.

CHAPTER NINE

Things Are Not Always as They Seem

So far, we have discussed strange things that happen in the practice of criminal law, but strange things happen to all of us in our non-work lives as well. I want to tell you a few stories that illustrate this point.

The first one was told to me by the priest who presided at my wedding to Charleen in 1968. (That makes fifty-six years and counting.) We had been married about two months when we invited Father to our apartment for dinner and he told us a story about the beginning of his ministry to illustrate doing your best even if things don't turn out as you intended and keeping a sense of humor through it all.

The second story concerns a sticky HR problem I caused at my law firm. When I was single, I always feared making two dates for the same night. Now as a senior partner in the law firm, I managed to employ two secretaries and only had one job.

Finally, I will tell you a story told to me by the medical director of a hospital where I served on the board of directors. While his gruff exterior projected an inpatient man who did not suffer fools lightly, he was truly one of the most caring and dedicated people I ever met. He told the story during the board meeting when the physicians were fighting with administration and the discussion started to get heated. It's a story about caring about each other and how that caring makes a difference in life. He got through to both sides at that meeting, and in fact, a tear or two could be seen in the eyes of a few of the attendees.

The Priest's Tale

He stood six feet, two inches tall and weighed 255 pounds, an imposing figure. Some would say intimidating. However, one look at his smiling countenance and his sparkling blue eyes topped off by a shock of red hair gave you a sense of peacefulness.

He could have been cast to lead the next St. Patrick's Day parade, leading thousands of marchers down New York City's Fifth Avenue. Perhaps the only thing that could keep this giant leprechaun from becoming the grand marshal was his name ... Dante Giuseppe Pusateri.

Father Dante was a fount of stories and told at least one during every sermon. Over a bowl of pasta and a few glasses of Chianti, he shared a story that he couldn't tell in church:

> My first assignment was to Saint Lucy's parish located on 102nd Street and Second Avenue in New York City. Back in the mid-1930s, this area

of the city—called Harlem—was for all intents and purposes a ghetto inhabited by Italian immigrants and their children. Indeed, three generations often lived in the same tenement or next door to each other. It was a tight-knit community and despite being 100-percent Italian, I stood out in a neighborhood of dark olive-skinned Italians. I even had to explain to members of our congregation that my family came from a small town located outside the city of Naples called the Agerola. For centuries, Naples was a thriving seaport and people from Ireland, Denmark, Norway and Germany eventually made it their home. Over the years, the intermixing of these nationalities provided offspring with fair skin, blue eyes and red or blonde hair.

I had been in this new parish for only four days when the pastor asked me to cover the wake service for Luca Rapetti at the Cinquemani Funeral Home around the corner from the church. Neither of the priests nor many of the Italian mourners—aside from the deceased's family—liked the traditional wake service, yet it was part of Italian tradition. A proper Italian wake had to be held for exactly three days, followed by the funeral mass at St. Lucy's. This in and of itself was a daunting task for the pall bearers because the church was on the second floor of the building and required a ninety-degree turn at the first landing.

The dearly departed's family gathered each day at the funeral home from two to five in the afternoon and then from seven to ten at night to receive family and friends. Of course, the deceased was there laid out in an open coffin. No matter how poor the deceased was, men were always dressed in a tuxedo and ladies wore pastel evening gowns. Going out in style was something you had to do. You also needed the traditional floral arrangements to surround the casket. The spouse would always have a six-foot floral arrangement made of white carnations with red roses diagonally placed in the "bleeding heart" arrangement. The children would always purchase the floral arrangement known as "the clock." This was a six-foot floral arrangement generally of gladioli in the center with a paper clockface, the hands pointing towards the guest of honor's time of death.

To help defray the cost of this affair, the family appointed one of their number, usually the oldest grandson or nephew, to receive the envelopes from those who attended. It was easy for mourners to identify this individual because he would be walking around the room clutching a fistful of white envelopes. Lastly, the funeral parlor would be arranged in a prescribed manner. There would be four to eight rows of folding chairs, depending on the deceased's popularity, with high-backed chairs or couches in the row closest to the casket for the family. I would appear at precisely 7:30 to say prayers for the departed and then lead five decades of the Rosary.

After the final blessing of the deceased and those in attendance, I would speak briefly to the family members in the front row.

At the Rapetti wake, after consoling the family, I noticed an individual in the traditional black garb of a grieving widow sitting off to the side. She looked so alone and afraid sitting by herself. I just had to go to try to comfort her. I know I don't look Italian, but I wanted to connect with her in a very special way. I walked over to her and knelt down next to her, and in my best Italian, I said: 'Mio caro. Non sembrare cosi triste. Tuo marito e con Dio, I suoi angeli e suoi santi.' (Translation: My dear. Don't look so sad. Your husband is with God, his angels, and his saints.)

She replied in her best English. 'Father, he was a no-good son of a bitch when he was alive, and he is a no-good son of a bitch now that he's dead.'

Rest in Peace, Luca. Wherever you are.

Looking for Love in All the Wrong Places

We had been together for almost six years. She came in one day, closed the door and said, "I'm leaving!"

This was not the end of a marriage but just as devastating, a six-year working relationship with the best secretary I ever had. Lisa Hanson was truly my go-to person. I was of the generation in which boys didn't learn to type, so I dictated my correspondence. Her office skills were superior. But more than that, she was intelligent and cared about her job, which to her was making me look good. My partners joked she knew what I was going to say before I said it and was finishing my sentences just like we were an old married couple. While we never had a social relationship outside the usual office functions, we considered ourselves more than colleagues. We were friends, even though I was probably twenty years older, and we shared a lot of the same interests except for music. She was Van Halen; I was more Alabama.

Once I recovered from my shock, I asked Lisa if there was anything I could do to get her to stay. As a senior partner in the law firm, I had some juice I could use to get a raise if that was the problem. She said it wasn't about the money. It seems that although she had an active social life, she was still living at home and wanted to expand her horizons by getting a job in a New York City law firm and an apartment there. After a little more digging, we got to the nub of the situation. Namely, she had yet to find somebody she felt she could spend the rest of her life with on Long Island, and perhaps New York City would be where she would find her Prince Charming. She told me that she would be leaving in four weeks, and she would help hire a replacement. In fact, she had already dictated the job ad to be placed in the *New York Law Journal*. We showed it to the office manager and got the approval to run the ad at once.

Cases You Can't Make Up

Within a week we had fifteen résumés that Lisa went over with a fine-toothed comb. Out of the fifteen, she thought three would be right for me, and we set up interviews. We hit paydirt with the first applicant, Margie Grant, who was currently employed in a small four-person law firm in Huntington and was looking for a change. Our fifty-five-attorney firm had everything she was looking for, including a nice pay increase for being a senior partner's secretary. Lisa had two weeks left with the firm and offered to help Margie learn the ropes and my idiosyncrasies. Without any prodding on my part, the ladies agreed that for the next four or five days Lisa would stay past 5 p.m. and Margie would come to our firm right after she finished her job to learn the ropes.

About six weeks after Lisa left, I received a telephone call on my private line, and I was happy to hear her voice once again. But I immediately noticed a problem in her voice—when you know somebody very well you can just tell by the cadence if there's a problem. And there was. After about thirty seconds she asked me if I would write a letter of recommendation for her. I remember commenting how backwards some of the big New York City firms were when they were looking for a recommendation after she had been at the job for over a month. Then, for the first time, I heard Lisa crying, "I hate the job and the commute. The people were completely standoffish. I was not used to being treated like that, and I quit a week ago. I'm now looking for a job back on Long Island."

I told her not to do anything until she heard back from me. I immediately went to the office manager, Anne Devereaux, and told her what happened. I had never pulled rank as a senior partner, but on this occasion, I felt I had to. I wanted Lisa back, but I didn't want to hurt Margie, who left her job to come work for us.

Annie said, "Leave it to me, and I'll speak to the managing partner." The decision made was simple: Tell Margie the truth.

We proposed that if Margie agreed, Lisa would return to the office as my secretary, and Margie would become a floating secretary working for partners and other lawyers whose secretaries were on vacation or out ill. We agreed to keep her salary at the same level and give her the first opportunity to work for a partner when a position became available. Anne told Margie the final decision would be hers. Margie asked for some time to think about it, and the next morning she told us, "It was clear to me from the beginning that Gregg and Lisa were a fantastic team. While I'm not happy about becoming a floater, I like working here. I also like Lisa, and I think they should be back together."

And so, Lisa came back to the firm. I was surprised to see there was no animosity between Lisa and Margie. I had thought that even though Margie took the high road, she still would harbor resentment towards Lisa for the double cross, but I never was able to figure out women.

About three months after Lisa was back, I found out that she and Margie went to the opening of a new bar in Farmingdale. Since it was opening weekend, it was predictably crowded. During the night, Lisa saw a good-looking young guy waving at them. He made his way through the crowd, walked up to Margie and gave her a big hug and kiss. Lisa thought that he was the boyfriend Margie often talked about.

Then Margie turned to Lisa and said, "I'd like you to meet my favorite cousin, Vincent Goff. Everybody calls him Jerry."

A year later, Lisa and Margie were partying again. This time, Margie was the maid of honor at Lisa and Jerry's wedding.

Lisa finally met her Prince Charming through the most circuitous route possible.

I guess you can't look for love. Love has to come and find you.

'An Act of Kindness, No Matter How Small, Is Never Wasted' – *Aesop*

While Micah Fishman had all the required degrees and licenses to be called "doctor," I think of him more as a physician. To me, being a doctor is a job, while being a physician is a calling in which you put the welfare of the patient above all else.

By the mid-1980s, doctors were complaining they were working harder and making less money thanks to health maintenance organizations and reduced Medicare reimbursements. They also hated doing all the documentation required by the insurance carriers to be paid. Malpractice rates were on the rise, and the pedestal the rest of us put doctors on when we were growing up seemed not so high as it once was. In short, doctors were an angry lot. It's not that doctors didn't take care of the patients—they did—but they did so with an attitude: let me get in and out of that exam room as fast as possible so I can see the next patient.

Clearly Micah was a physician, but also, and more importantly, he was a mensch, Yiddish for "a person of integrity and honor," qualities Micah Fishman personified. Let me explain.

As a trustee of a community hospital, I knew I should have spent time around the hospital in places other than the boardroom, but I never did until I was appointed to the performance improvement (PI) committee. As a member of the PI committee, I got to see firsthand where our hospital ranked in comparison to its peers, what metrics we needed to meet for Medicare reimbursement and how to address "any unintended, adverse or undesirable development in a patient's condition," which had to be reported to the New York State Health Department. At our monthly meetings, we reviewed incident reports and in consultation with the hospital's quality assurance team tried to improve the process to avoid future issues.

I decided the time had come to go on hospital rounds with one of the doctors. When I was a student, I was never smart enough to even think about medical school. However, I had become a medical buff in my legal career, learning just enough medicine to be able to defend my clients before the New York State Health Department's Office of Professional Medical

Conduct. I read medical texts, did research on the internet and spoke to teaching physicians with whom I had a relationship. Yet with all this book knowledge, I had never spoken to our hospitalized patients, heard about their illness or learned how they were treated.

It was a no-brainer to ask the ever-energetic Dr. Fishman, who also served as the hospital's medical director, if I could accompany him on rounds. He graciously agreed. One Saturday afternoon, we started our rounds. Because Micah only had four patients in the hospital that day, he had time to give me a doctor's tour of our hospital.

"Here's where it all starts," he said as we blasted through the two swinging doors stenciled EMERGENCY ROOM in large bright-red letters.

Micah spoke to the charge nurse, whom he addressed by her first name. Courtney responded by saying it was a slow day and although there were seven people in the ER waiting room, all were triaged and considered "treat and release" patients. As we were about to run out of the ER (Micah's walk was about twice the speed of a normal pace), he stopped in front of the only occupied ER bay.

I saw a patch of hair just as white as the sheets covering the patient. Micah approached the bed and spoke to the patient, Estelle. He found out she was an eighty-eight-year-old from a local nursing home. She had no family in the area, her stomach felt better, and her doctor said she would see her on Monday. She also told him that she had been in the ER since early morning the previous day.

Micah, now wearing his medical director hat, found Estelle's chart and noted she was stable and there was an order from the ER house doctor to discharge her to the second floor medical-surgical unit. The note was dated Friday 2:20 p.m. It was now 12:10 p.m. Saturday, and Estelle was still in the ER.

So why was she still in the ER bay instead of a hospital room where she could get scheduled nursing care? Both Micah and I knew from the PI committee report given at last Tuesday's meeting that we had only 72-percent occupancy on the med-surg floor.

After Micah spoke with Courtney, he called the director of nursing and requested that Estelle be given a room at once. The discussion turned a bit hotter when he raised his voice and replied, "No, she's not my patient, but what does that have to do with it? She's been in the ER for more than twenty-four hours when we have open beds upstairs. It's just not right." With those words, Micah ended the call.

Living Up to Your Name

Perhaps his parents had a premonition when they named him Micah, for as the quote from the Bible reads: "What does the Lord require of thee, but to do justly and to love mercy and to walk humbly with God." (Micah 6:8)

After telling Estelle he would see her later, we stormed out of the ER, taking the stairs.

"I don't wait for elevators," Micah said.

As we walked down the hall of the fourth floor to his patients' rooms, I watched him greet each RN, LPN and orderly like old friends. "I've only been doing this for twenty years," he responded when I observed he knew the name of everyone we met, including the janitor.

As we entered each patient's room, Micah introduced me as a hospital trustee and asked if he could tell me about their condition and allow me to observe his exam. The patients readily agreed and appreciated the interest the hospital had in their condition by sending me to visit.

Then back to the stairwell for the trip down to the first floor. When we arrived at the first-floor landing, I headed to the parking lot exit when Micah said, "One more stop." In response to my quizzical look he said, "Back to the ER."

As we got closer, I sensed Micah was getting ready for a fight. Blasting through the ER doors again, he scanned the scene. "Where is Estelle?"

Courtney had a big smile on her face when she replied, "She's upstairs in room 213. Sorry, I could not get her a room earlier. I'm happy you did."

Mission accomplished. Micah did not know Estelle, but he cared about people as a physician should, but that's not where my story about Micah ends. It continues on a strip of desert in Saudi Arabia about thirty miles south of the border with Kuwait about five years later.

On August 2, 1990, units of the Iraqi Republican Guard crossed over the border and invaded Kuwait. The invasion, which lasted all of two days, was literally unopposed and the Iraqi army now controlled the rich oil fields of Kuwait. At the request of King Fahd of Saudi Arabia, on August 7, the United States began Operation Desert Shield. Shortly thereafter on August 22, President George H.W. Bush signed an order calling up selective reserve units. Micah Fishman was in one of those units.

That was the reason Dr. Fishman turned in his white coat for a camouflage battle dress uniform. Instead of a stethoscope hanging around his neck, he proudly wore his army dog tags, and a .45-caliber semiautomatic pistol strapped to his hip replaced the prescription pad he usually kept in his front pocket. The silver-threaded oak leaf worn on the middle of his shirt announced Micah's rank of lieutenant colonel, and his command consisted of 118 men and women who would set up a mobile army surgical hospital (MASH) unit in the desert. MASH units were designed to place medical personnel closer to the front lines so that wounded soldiers could be treated sooner and surgically, if required. Indeed, the concept proved most successful during the Korean War, when any soldier who made it to a MASH unit alive had a 97-percent chance of survival. Nurses, medical and lab techs and six other physicians, the majority of whom were trauma surgeons, served under Lt. Col. Fishman.

Micah 's unit arrived in Saudi Arabia on January 16, 1991. Tank Company 4 was twenty kilometers north of their location. The tank company consisted of three platoons of four tanks each with two additional tanks in headquarters, along with their support vehicles carrying mechanics, spare parts, fuel and ammo. The tanks were the best America had, the Abrams M1A2s. Each tank was manned by a four-person crew: a tank commander, gunner, loader and driver. The tank group arrived in theater on December 13 and spent Christmas Day in the desert forming a defensive wall by the Kuwaiti-Saudi border.

As Micah's MASH unit was gearing up, so did the air-war phase of Operation Desert Storm, which began on January 17. Clearly, the invasion would start soon, and the medical personnel of the unit worked vigorously to complete their mission of building a surgical hospital in the middle of the godforsaken desert.

By the first week of February, the field hospital was ready to accept its first patient, and the waiting began. It was about this time that Micah's second in command told him the captain of Tank Company 4 wished to pay his respects to the lieutenant colonel, and a meeting was set for 1300 hours on February 14.

As the appointed hour approached, the rumble of diesel engines and sight of sand flying on the horizon announced the impending arrival of the tank force commander. Captain Kyle O'Connor, a native of San Antonio, Texas, had graduated from Baylor University as an ROTC officer and spent five years in the army's armored division. As for the vast majority of soldiers in the desert, this was going to be his first taste of combat. Kyle and his men were well-trained, but like anyone else going into combat for the first time, they were fearful of the unknown. Besides making a courtesy call to the lieutenant colonel, O'Connor was on a spy mission. Specifically, he was asked by his fellow officers in the US Army Rangers unit attached to the Eighty-Second Airborne Division, both of which were going in on the first wave, to find out firsthand just how good the MASH unit was in case they needed its lifesaving help. That was the real reason O'Connor took his Abrams tank south.

After the obligatory salute and shop talk, Micah invited Kyle into his HQ tent for a private conversation. Micah had a genuine gift for getting people to open up, whether it was a patient who was giving him a detailed medical history while under the illusion he and the doctor were just BSing or a tank commander. Micah's caring personality soon had the young captain sharing his doubts, and yes, his fears.

"We've been on the frontline for eight weeks now. No electricity, little water for anything but drinking, and I fear my guys are losing their edge. We drill and train, but it's not like when we first got here. And I'm responsible for the lives of a hundred men, many of them just kids."

The words "just kids" were especially hard for Micah to hear when they came out of the mouth of a twenty-eight-year-old. Micah sensed Kyle was starting to have a morale problem with his men. The prescription Micah gave O'Connor was as simple as it was brilliant.

"Captain, on 18 February at 1200 hours we are going to have a barbecue right here at the hospital, and your men are invited."

The out-of-the-blue invitation stunned the young officer. Then Micah added, in a professional yet paternal tone, "The one thing you have to get through your men's thick heads is that 40 percent of my unit is female. We treat them like our sisters, and you will too. If any of your guys step out of line, I will personally shoot them."

O'Connor did not miss the fact that Micah's words were punctuated with several pats to his .45-caliber pistol. The captain must have been thinking, *This doctor needs a doctor. He is a certified looney.* Yet Micah had a way about him that instilled confidence, and the barbecue invitation (more accurately put, the order) was accepted. On the designated date and time, three-quarters of Captain O'Connor's tanks and support vehicles arrived at the MASH site. Hot dogs and hamburgers were cooked, and a few cases of soda pop (which allegedly bore the label Budweiser) were enjoyed; followed by a softball or volleyball game or—if you wanted—a personal tour of an Abrams battle tank. Six hours later the company left, and Micah did not have to make good on his threat to shoot anyone.

Then it finally came. The order was given that Tank Company Four would surprise the enemy by not going directly into Kuwait but by attacking in Iraq just to the west of the Kuwaiti border at 0400 hours on February 24. O'Connor had been briefed by his brigade's intelligence officer that their target was the First Hammurabi Division, an elite force that reported directly to Saddam Hussein. They were better equipped and better trained than the regular Iraqi troops, and it was the same division that six months earlier led the invasion into Kuwait. Now it would be American armor that would spearhead the attack allowing the Rangers and the Eighty-Second Airborne to follow.

An hour before the attack was to commence, O'Connor assembled the men of his fourteen tanks. Twenty-year-old tank drivers and crusty old first sergeants gathered around their captain. As part of his briefing, O'Connor reminded his men that once the infantry went through the hole in the enemy's line, their job then was to secure the line. The intelligence report, he advised the troops, expected the initial thrust of the attack to be the easy part of the mission. The real test would come when the Iraqis counterattacked to attempt to seal the breach and push the coalition forces back into Saudi Arabia and then head for its capital, Riyadh. The captain reminded his men that there was nothing in their sector between them and Riyadh except the MASH unit. O'Connor was quick to remind his men that the hospital had only their M16s and sidearms to defend itself.

"They don't even have a SAW (squad automatic weapon), and I don't think the Republican Guard will treat the nurses as their sisters."

His voice cracked as he finished that sentence. O'Connor saw Sergeant First Class Barry Peters stand and recognized his senior noncommissioned officer. The sergeant said, "Captain, we hear you loud and clear. Rest assured we won't let the bad guys get through. They'll never get near Micah, Jay, Alex, Andrew, Robin, Connie, Joanne ... not only are they American soldiers, but they're our friends."

Most assuredly, Company Four would have fought hard to protect the occupants of the hospital even if they had not known them by name. But thanks to Lt. Col. Micah Fishman, Company Four was not only defending Americans, they were defending "our friends."

And they did.

CHAPTER TEN

There Is an Author Inside of You

My wife and I were sitting on our front porch enjoying our 5 p.m. glass of cabernet, when we heard the unmistakable yips of Yorkshire terriers. Our neighbors, Kenna and Wyatt, were walking their two pups, who were directing their aggression at the senior male German shepherd in the fenced yard across the street. As Yorkies are wont to do, they were pulling at their leashes while the shepherd just looked at them and, no doubt, secretly laughed.

The Yorkies now directed their attention towards us and started to climb the five porch steps where my wife greeted them. In between playing with the two balls of fur, she managed to say a few words to Kenna.

I invited Wyatt into the house for a glass of wine. After discussing the current issues concerning our incompetent HOA, he asked what I had been doing to keep busy now that I was retired. I told him that in addition to volunteer work in the community and church, I was writing the fifth draft of the manuscript for my new book (yes, the book you just read). Wyatt was surprised to learn I had written a first book, and

I hastened to assure him that the marketing for *Scenes From a Criminal Lawyer's Notebook* would be much better.

While we discussed some of the stories in Volume One, it happened again. He told me a story of his own. Every time I would give a talk on my book to a large senior-citizen community or small book club, as I would be packing to leave, one or two people would come up to tell me things that had happened in their lives—things that would also be worthy of a book. After a brief discussion, my advice is always the same: "Just go do it."

Wyatt, however, presented a bigger problem. He told me that Kenna's great-great-grandfather served in the Twenty-Sixth North Carolina Regiment during the Civil War and fought at the Battle of Gettysburg and that her great-grandfather had collected letters and newspaper articles from that time in a binder of materials on her family history.

"Kenna's grandfather, who inherited the material from his father, added more letters and stuff about their family, and now we have two crammed four-inch binders. Granddad was supposed to compile the information and write a book to be handed down to future generations. Of course, he never did so. Neither did Kenna's mom when she inherited the material. All she did was add more stuff to the binders. Now that her mom is in her mid-nineties, it won't be long before Kenna and I get the binders. I've told Kenna we should just throw them out in the trash, but she insists I get them shredded."

"Blasphemy" was the first word that popped into my mind, and it came out of my mouth with such force that I believe I startled him.

"What do you expect me to do? I'm no author," Wyatt said in self-defense.

And that took us down a thread I shared with Wyatt and would like to share with you, because perhaps, just perhaps, there is something in the back of your mind telling you to put your thoughts down on paper.

I'm a storyteller. The classic elements of a story—characters, plot, conflict, etc.—are already there as I commit my experiences to paper. My task is to make what starts out as an ordinary event into a meaningful and interesting story that reinforces the shared humanity of the writer and reader.

History teaches us that cultures have told stories going back to the cave drawings in Lascaux and Chauvet, France. We all have a story to tell. Just think about something you wish to share. Just like those cave dwellers, there must be something you would like to leave as a legacy.

We are not all as fortunate as Wyatt and Kenna to have a collection of papers providing a hundred or more years of family history. But we all have a history, an oral history, that will disappear unless we decide to pass it down.

In my case, I did not make that decision. It was made for me by my Aunt Mary. When you went to visit her, the first thing you had to do was eat. First came the antipasto, followed by wine, followed by pasta, followed by more wine. The wine, of course, was homemade by Uncle Arthur and served in small juice glasses. Not many glasses needed to be served before the stories started.

The stories my aunt and other relatives told were about their childhoods. They were born in the United States but went back to Italy and grew up in the small farming town of Agerola, located just north of Naples. Most of the stories were about my grandmother's family, but we could go back as far as grandma's mother. At one of our family dinners, Aunt Mary looked at me and said it's about time somebody writes down the stories. If not, they would be lost forever "and you are that somebody."

As Aunt Mary requested, I took notes at the dinner table about the stories she and the other family elders told us. Then came the hard part of writing the stories. The temptation was to take the easy way out—just jot down the notes, compile them as they were told to you, staple the pages together and call it "Family History."

That's a mistake. Nobody's interested in your diary unless your name is Anne Frank. The key is to make the stories you heard interesting. Yes, you may have to embellish some of the parts or fill in the blanks to make the story readable. Remember, you want to make your relatives pick up the book and read it.

Your goal is to pass a priceless heirloom down to your future family. Somebody has to do it, and Aunt Mary would tell you, "You are that somebody."

Everyone has a story, and we all have the storyteller's gene.

So what holds people back? Perhaps there are several reasons, ranging from laziness to being too busy to just not knowing where to start. I can't fix laziness or give you more than twenty-four hours in a day, but I can answer the question about where you should start.

First of all, remember as a human being, you're a natural storyteller. You want to tell stories that mean something to you and pass them on to your family and friends and just maybe other people would hear about what you are doing and want to read the stories as well. You have to keep the story interesting.

As I told you at the beginning, my stories are semi-true. To me that means the kernel of the story actually happened. I know the kernel of the story is real because it happened to me, or I spoke to people who had firsthand experience concerning the topic. You have the skill to master taking that kernel and make popcorn out of it. Better still, caramel popcorn.

We all have the experiences—some sad and some funny, some mundane, some unbelievable—and all you need to do is get those thoughts onto a sheet of shiny white paper.

The odds are, you're never going to be an author whose book appears on the *New York Times* bestseller list. But who really cares? That's not your goal. Your goal is to leave a tangible and enjoyable record of your family for those that will follow you. If you fail to do so, in two or three generations, all the stories you know about your family and what you did in your life will be erased from the world forever. Not out of any malice, but because nobody will know about them.

That's why you can give yourself, your family and just maybe the world a priceless gift.

It's up to you now. Just go do it.

ACKNOWLEDGMENTS

As I said in my first books, it really takes a village to produce an independently published book. The process seems never ending! After you complete your first draft—called a "vomit draft"—where you put down all of your ideas, you edit.

You just don't edit once. You go through three or four drafts before you have a manuscript you're not embarrassed to share. Then you commence your search to find unsuspecting friends to read your manuscript, looking for typos and content flaws. This is a critical step because you can read and reread your own manuscript and still gloss over obvious errors, especially if you don't type and rely on dictation software.

Thanks to Patrick Service; Carolyn Hriso; the Sandys; Barbara Shevelson; and my colleagues at the CAP Team, Maryann Wolf; Robin Lane; and Dan Marusa for sharing your time and efforts on this venture.

Occasionally, lightning strikes when you're working on a book, as it did when I met George Higgins at a Christmas party. He just happens to be a professor of English composition. I learned more from his edits than any English course I ever took in school.

Lastly, this book could not be possible without the help of two ladies who were with me on my first book and decided to help on this project, my copy editor and book designer, Kelly Lojk, and the chef who takes the ingredients of what you have written and turns it into a book, my editor and publisher, Nora Gaskin Esthimer.

Thanks to all my villagers and everyone who encouraged me to write this book. You're all great.

A FAVOR, PLEASE

I trust you enjoyed *Scenes From a Criminal Lawyer's Notebook: Cases You Can't Make Up* as much as I did sharing my stories with you.

Fifty percent of the profit from the sale of this book will be donated to the V Foundation for Cancer Research based in Cary, North Carolina. The foundation has an endowment to cover all administrative expenses, so 100% of all donations will go directly to cancer research.

You can make this donation more meaningful by:

✦ Telling your friends about the book
✦ Leaving an honest review at amazon.com and goodreads.com
✦ Posting your comments about the book on social media
✦ Suggesting the book to your reading group

I am also available to meet with your group or book club via Zoom or in person to provide additional information about my stories and how you can start writing a book.

For more information, contact me at
gnacbooks.com

Apple users, please use **https://gnacbooks.com**

Thanks for your help and God bless.
– Gregg

www.ingramcontent.com/pod-product-compliance
Lightning Source LLC
Chambersburg PA
CBHW070615030426
42337CB00020B/3806